Muhammadan Education

IN

Bengal

Muhammadan Education

IN

Bengal.

BY

ABDUL KARIM, B. A.

GYAN

Published by

Gyan Publishing House
5, Ansari Road
Daryaganj, New Delhi-110002
Phone: 011-47034999, 9811692060
E-mail: books@gyanbooks.com

Distribution Network
gyanbooks.com
India, USA, Canada, UK, Australia

ISBN: 978-81-212-8456-1 (HB)
First Published, 1900

2nd Impression 2024

Printed at: Gyan Press, Delhi.

MUHAMMADAN EDUCATION IN BENGAL
Author: ABDUL KARIM

Muhammadan Education

IN

Bengal.

(ORIGINALLY WRITTEN FOR THE MUHAMMADAN EDUCATIONAL CONFERENCE, AND PUBLISHED IN A REVISED FORM).

BY

ABDUL KARIM B. A.

Assistant Inspector of Schools, Bengal, Member of the Asiatic Society, Fellow of the Calcutta University.

METCALFE PRESS : CALCUTTA.

1900.

CONTENTS.

Muhammadan Education.

IN

BENGAL.

CHAPTER I.

NEGLECT OF ENGLISH EDUCATION.

Every student of Indian History knows how and when Bengal passed into the hands of the English nation. The system of Government, known in history as "dual administration," in which the Nawab Nazim took a prominent part, lasted only a short time. But the Persian language continued to be used in Courts for nearly a century longer.

With the fall of the Musalman empire in 1757 the seats of learning which supplied government officials, disappeared. It was necessary, therefore, to establish an institution to qualify Musalmans in Bengal for the public service. Warren Hastings, the far-sighted statesman who was the "administrative organiser" of the British Indian Empire, established the Calcutta Madrasah in the year 1782. The original intention of the founder was "to promote the study of the Arabic and Persian languages and of Muhammadan Law, with a view more especially to the production of qualified officers for the Courts of Justice." The principal subjects prescribed for study were Natural Philosophy, Theology, Law, Astronomy, Geometry, Arithmetic, Logic, Rhetoric, Oratory and Grammar. For about half a century the successful students of the Madrasah monopolised almost all the judicial and executive posts under Government, and they predominated at the Bar. Justice had all along been administered in India in the language of the conquerors. From the beginning of their rule Persian was the official language of the Musalman rulers. The Hindus readily learnt Persian and some of them even became teachers thereof. The English continued the use of Persian in courts so as to make as little change at first as possible. But in due course Persian gave way to the Indian Vernaculars and English as the Court Languages of British India.

Our utilitarian fellow-countrymen, the Hindus, quick to perceive the immense advantage which a knowledge of English literature and science would give them, early devoted themselves to western studies. Although the Government of India did not pass any definite legislative measure dealing with education after receiving the first Educational Despatch from the Court of Directors in 1814, the advanced section of the Hindu community, under the guidance of the celebrated patriot and linguist, Raja Rammohan Ray, and the philanthropic watch-maker, Mr. David Hare, established, as early as 1816, an institution called "Vidyalaya" for the education of Hindu children in the English language and literature. In the course of a few years a taste for English was widely disseminated and independent schools, conducted by young men educated in the "Vidyalaya" sprang up in every direction. The tide thus set in strongly in favour of English education.

When Lord William Bentinck was Governor-General of India a controversy arose as to whether the oriental languages or English should be the medium of education for the people of India. There was a great agitation among the advocates of oriental learning and the authorities were influenced by this. Finding that a decision was likely to be come to in favour of Oriental learning, Raja Rammohan Ray and Mr. David Hare, the pioneers of English education in India, submitted a very strong representation in favour of the introduction of English and they succeeded in persuading Lord William Bentinck to acquiesce in their views. Dr. Duff, the most celebrated missionary educationist of the time, also took a prominent part in the agitation for the introduction of English. Lord Macaulay, at that time a member of the Governor-General's Council, wrote his celebrated Minute, and Lord William Bentinck passed the memorable Resolution of the Government of India in March 1835, in favour of English education.

Whilst the Hindus were thus showing readiness, zeal and generosity towards the spread of English education in India, far different were the feelings of the Musalmans, whose attitude towards English education was anything but friendly. When it was proposed to appropriate the whole of Government Educational grants to English education, there was a petition against it from the Musalmans of Calcutta, signed by about 8000 persons, including all the learned and respectable Muhammadan gentlemen of this city. They regarded the introduction of English as a step towards conversion to Christianity. This hostile attitude of the Musalmans towards English education stands in strong contrast to the attitude of the Hindu community, and accounts for the vast disparity in English education between the two communities, which indeed still subsists.

There was no real cause for this suspicion, for, the Government had declared, as early as 1808, the policy of religious neutrality. But the Musalmans thought that they had reason to be suspicious. It must be admitted that the Government could not help taking an extreme position in this controversy. It was necessary to advocate either English education or Oriental. Yet it is a pity that room could not have been found for both. Had Oriental learning found a place in the curriculum of the English schools and colleges, as at present, most probably there would not have been misapprehension. But unfortunately it was decided that the object of the British Government was to be "the promotion of European Literature and Science among the natives of India, and that all the funds appropriated for the purpose of education would be best employed on English education alone." The exclusive study of a foreign language and the total neglect of the classical and vernacular languages of the people not unnaturally created suspicion, the result of which, as will be shown later on, has proved detrimental to the interests of my co-religionists. The advocates of English education seem to have overshot their mark, when Lord Macaulay, as their mouth-piece, declared, with his characteristic facility for exaggeration, that "a single shelf of a good European library was worth the whole native literature of India and Arabia." Dr. Duff in describing the "Ocean of Oriental literature" quoted Ferdausi's satire on the court of Ghazni, "The magnificent court of Ghazni is a sea without bottom and without shore, I have fished in it long, but have found no pearl." Arabic, Persian, and Sanskrit, held by the people in great reverence as the only source of wisdom, were in consequence of such teachings looked upon with unconcealed contempt by those who were receiving English education. Moreover, the effect produced by the exclusive study of English was at first far from satisfactory. The first generation of Indian students of English Literature, who learnt English along with their classical languages, consisted of sound, substantial and self-made men with definite religious views and high character. The next generation, the first fruits of exclusive education in a foreign language, consisted of men of a different type. The students of Shakespeare and Milton could scarcely spell their names in their own mother-tongue. Not being grounded in their ancestral theology and traditions these men were infected with scepticism; and the morals of educated Bengalis suffered in consequence. Indeed the Hindu society of the time presented the appearance of chaos. The orthodoxy of the Hindus was seriously affected and their national characteristics were also, to some extent, affected. Some of the most intelligent English scholars of the time did not hesitate to embrace Christianity. All these circumstances, viz. the exclusive study of English with a total disregard of oriental learning, the lowering of morals, and the effect on manners due to the exclusively secular education imparted through a foreign language, and the conversion to Christianity of some of the students, rightly or wrongly attributed thereto, could not but alarm a religious people like the Musalmans. Consequently they, for the most part, kept aloof from English education.

But, as I have already said, there was nothing in the motives of Government to justify this alarm. We believe that it was a mistake to exclude altogether from the course of studies the classical languages of the people. But this did not affect what had been the policy from the very beginning, viz. religious neutrality. Government never adopted a proselytising policy. It was very wisely decided that English education in India should be purely secular. The report that Government had a proselytising purpose in its educational policy had no foundation in fact. Indeed the English Government has proved a great blessing to the Musalmans as well as to all other nationalities inhabiting this country. There are not many countries even in Europe where protection of life and property is so complete as in India and where there is so little interference, on the part of Government, with personal liberty, or with freedom in the public expression of opinion in matters of politics and religion. There is peace throughout the land and the good of the people is the paramount object of the Government. If Lord Curzon were to ask all the educated and enlightened people of India, as he asked the Municipal Commissioners of Jubbalpur "Is there at this moment a Government in the world that, if it were in our place, would devote its resources both of means and men, with so large-hearted a munificence to your relief, and would identify itself so thoroughly with the people?" he would receive only one reply and that, as he presumed, in the negative. This however, is not the place to recount the blessings of British rule.

Experience should have taught the Musalman leaders that the Musalmans had less cause to fear conversion through education than any other community in India. Islam is founded on principles that are too strong to be easily shaken. It has been less affected by western education and civilisation than any other system. The Musalmans could have given their children religious education at home and then sent them to English schools for secular education, when there was no longer any doubt about the motives of Government. Had the Musalmans been wise they would have perceived the advantage of the change and adapted themselves to the exigencies of the time. But an "ancient conquering race cannot easily divest itself of the traditions of its nobler days." The Musalmans, confident of the superiority of their system of education, continued to pursue their old studies with the lamentable result that before long they were practically excluded from that share of office and emolument in Government service which they once monopolised.

About the year 1830 a proposal was made by the Government to administer justice in India through the English language. But the Court of Directors decided that justice should be administered in the language of the people. Subsequently it was decided that the proceedings of the higher courts should be conducted in English and those of the lower courts in the vernacular languages of the various provinces. As the great majority of the people did not know how to read and write, steps had to be taken to educate them. A Department of education was established and primary and secondary schools were set up. As the Musalmans kept themselves aloof from the recognised system of education, no special attention appears to have been given to their wants and requirements. The schools were under Hindu management, they were almost exclusively attended by Hindu pupils, the teachers were Hindus and instruction was imparted through the medium of Bengali

CHAPTER II.

DIFFICULTY OF THE MUSALMANS OF BENGAL IN LEARNING LANGUAGES.

The Musalmans of the North-Western Provinces and the Punjab are not likely to realise the great disadvantages of their co-religionists in Bengal with regard to learning languages. Properly speaking the Musalmans of Bengal have no particular language of their own, as their district dialect does not deserve to be called by this name. The assumption that Bengali is the vernacular of all the Musalmans of Bengal is not wholly correct. In the large towns many Musalmans speak Urdu, while in the Mufussil the mother-tongue of the respectable Musalmans is a kind of Bengali which is different from pure Bengali.

The Musalmans of Bengal may be divided into two classes, viz. Musalmans by descent and Musalmans by conversion. Those among the former who have not had occasion to come frequently in contact with their Hindu neighbours, speak as their forefathers did ; while those who have been living for generations in close contact with Hindus have adopted their mode of speaking, but they still retain a strong predilection for the study of their classical languages. The converts and their descendants, on the other hand, speak more like their Hindu forefathers, and have little inclination for the study of the classical languages of their co-religionists. Hence the Musalmans of those places that are largely inhabited by Musalmans by descent generally attach much importance to Urdu, Persian, and Arabic, while the Musalmans of places largely inhabited by converts, care very little for these languages.

Thus it will be seen that the respectable Musalmans of Bengal have to learn more or less five languages, viz. Arabic and Persian, the languages of their Scriptures and Literature,

Urdu, the language of their society, and Bengali and English, the languages of the Courts. It is this that stands, to a great extent, in the way of fair competition with other classes of people, who have to learn two or three languages only. Though Urdu is not the vernacular of the Musalmans of Bengal, it is regarded as their national language—their *lingua franca* by which they communicate with their co-religionists all over India. The acquirement of this language is, therefore, considered to be an essential accomplishment for every respectable Musalman. This is one of the reasons why respectable Musalmans prefer that their children should be educated through the medium of Urdu. The lower classes generally imitate the gentry in matters of education. They naturally prefer to teach their children a language the acquirement of which is likely to raise their social status. There is another reason for the preference of Urdu. Many of the religious books of the Musalmans have been translated from Arabic into Urdu. Those who cannot afford to teach their children Arabic, content themselves with teaching them Urdu, through which they may learn the fundamental principles of their religion and traditions. Perhaps there is no other religion, the ignorant and illiterate followers of which care so much for their faith as Musalmans of their corresponding position do for Islam. The peasants quitting their ploughs and saying their prayers in the fields, the labourers prostrating themselves in the streets when the time of prayer comes, are sights too common to need any mention. Indeed the Prophet of Arabia inspired his followers with a religious ferver almost unexampled in the annals of Religion. Islam governs every Musalman's actions, pervades his thoughts, conversation, business dealings, and conduct of every day life. To the Musalmans education means first religious education, secondly moral education and lastly professional education. They first of all think of teaching their children a language through the medium of which they may receive religious instruction. I wish it was, as in the case of the Musalmans of North-Western Provinces and the Punjab, the vernacular language of the province. The Musalmans of Bengal would not have then to labour under such great disadvantages. Bengali is the mother-tongue of our fellow-countrymen the Hindus ; moreover, their one object is "to qualify their children for an official or professional career." While ordinary primary schools were, therefore, adapted to the wants of the Hindu community, they did not meet the requirements of the Musalmans, with whom "the teaching of the mosque must precede the lessons of the school." The Hindus had little difficulty in mastering their mother-tongue and, as has been shown, they readily learnt English. They soon filled almost all the posts to which natives of India were admitted and rose in power and prosperity. The Musalmans, on the contrary, lost even what they had, and gradually declined in every respect.

CHAPTER III.

REPORTS AND RESOLUTIONS ON MUHAMMADAN EDUCATION.

The deplorable state of things stated above seems to have remained almost unnoticed till recent years. At last it attracted the attention of English statesmen who began to discuss the subject. Mr. E. C. Bayley C. S. I. writes thus "Is it any subject for wonder that they held aloof from a system which, however good in itself, made no concession to their prejudices, made in fact no provision for what they esteemed their necessities, and which was in its nature unavoidably antagonistic to their interests, and at variance with their social traditions." Sir William Hunter writes in rather strong language thus "The language of our Government schools in Lower Bengal is Hindu and the masters are Hindus. The Musal-

I A

mans with one consent spurned the instructions of idolators through the medium of idolatry...the astute Hindu has covered the country with schools adapted to the wants of his own community, but wholly unsuited to the Muhammadans......Our rural schools seldom enable a Muhammadan to learn the tongue necessary for his holding a respectable position in life and for the performance of his religious duties." These and similar remarks made by those who had carefully enquired into the subject attracted the notice of Government and the Earl of Mayo dealt with it in an exhaustive Resolution in 1871. "It is evident," says the Resolution, "from the statistics received by the Government that in no part of the country, except perhaps in the North-Western Provinces and the Punjab, do the Muhammadans adequately or in proportion to the rest of the community, avail themselves of the educational advantages that the Government offers." His Excellency directed "that further and more systematic encouragement and recognition should be given to the classical and vernacular languages of the Muhammadans in all Government schools and colleges; that in avowedly English schools established in Muhammadan districts the appointment of qualified English teachers should be encouraged; that assistance should be given by grants-in-aid to enable them to open schools of their own, and that greater encouragement should be given to the creation of a vernacular Literature for Muhammadans—a measure the importance of which was specially urged upon the Government of India by Her Majesty's Secretary of State on more than one occasion." This Resolution was communicated to the Local Governments and Administrations.

On receipt of reports from the Local Governments and Administrations, Lord Northbrook came to the conclusion "that wherever the ordinary vernacular of the country was read and written in the Hindustani or the Urdu character there Muhammadans occupied their proper position in the primary and secondary schools. In the North-Western Provinces, in Oudh and in the Punjab the attendance of Muhammadans in the lower and middle schools is, on the whole, rather above than below the proportion which Muhammadans bear to the total population." The reports all agreed that the existing system had not succeeded in attracting the Musalmans to the higher branches of education. It was found that "the Musalmans are not so much averse to the subjects which the English Government has decided to teach as to the modes or machinery through which instruction is offered." His Excellency held that "many of the drawbacks to the universality of the educational system are susceptible of removal, since to the traditions and reasonable hesitation which keep aloof the Muhammadans are added certain obstacles which the system itself interposes by using a language that is unfamiliar and a machinery that is uncongenial." His Excellency admitted "the desirability of framing a series of high class text-books to encourage the publication of valuable Muhammadan works, and to offer prizes either for good translations of foreign works or for original studies." In concluding the Resolution His Excellency expressed the hope "that in all provinces where Muhammadans were few and often exposed to all the disadvantages which affect a religious minority without wealth or influence, it would be the special care of Government to satisfy themselves that these endeavours to encourage the education of Muhammadans would be persistently maintained."

This Resolution was carefully considered by the Local Governments and steps were taken in the desired direction by some of them. The Government of Madras, notwithstanding the contrary opinions expressed by the Director of Public Instruction and the Syndicate of the Madras University, was convinced "that the existing scheme of instruction was framed with too exclusive reference to the requirements of the Hindu students, and that Muhammadans were placed at so great a disadvantage that the wonder was not that the Muhammadan element in the schools was so small but that it existed at all." Some important steps were accordingly taken for the spread and encouragement of Muhammadan Education in the Madras Presidency. In other provinces also similar action was taken.

The educational statistics of the time, we are speaking of, showed that while the Musalmans of Bengal numbered more than 32 per cent of the total population, their proportion to the total number in schools known to the Department was only 14·4 per cent. This disproportion was still more conspicuous in the colleges where only 4 per cent of the pupils belonged to the Muhammadan community. In reviewing these statistics the Director of Public Instruction, Bengal, remarked (in his report for 1871-72) "The Musalmans have fallen behind the time, and require still the inducements held out forty years ago to the whole community, but of which only Hindus availed themselves. Such, however, has been the progress of education and the influence of the grant-in-aid system in promoting self-help that the encouragement which was then considered just and right would now be called downright bribery. Still unless the strong inducements in general use forty years ago are held out to Muhammadans now I have little hope of seeing them drawn to our schools." The Government of Bengal, however, decided that it was not necessary to establish special schools for Muhammadans. As the vernacular of the mass of Musalmans in Bengal was known to be Bengali, the ordinary Patshalas of the country were held to supply the proper means of elementary education. But it was admitted that schools of all classes might be made more attractive by increasing the number of Muhammadan officers in the various grades of the Department, especially in Muhammadan districts.

A few years later a proposal was made to connect the Maktabs throughout Bengal with the institutions for higher Muhammadan education in Calcutta and other places. The attempt, however, proved a failure, and it was abandoned in favour of an opposite policy which was expressed in the hope that the Maktabs "might be gradually moulded into true primary schools." Endeavours have been made to carry out this policy, but without much success. Of the many thousand

Maktabs in Bengal only a few have adopted the Departmental standards.

One very important step, however, was taken at that time, and this has done a good deal for Muhammadan education in Bengal. The Mohsin Endowment was set free for the encouragement and extension of education among the Musalmans of Bengal. It may not be out of place to give a short history of this endowment. In the year 1806, a Muhammadan gentleman of the *Shia* sect died, leaving an estate yielding Rs. 45,000 per annum, in trust for "pious uses." The deed of trust appointed two trustees, to each of whom a share of the proceeds, amounting to one-ninth, was assigned. Three-ninths were assigned to certain specific objects, viz. the performance of certain religious rites and ceremonies, and the repair of an *Imambarah* while the remaining four-ninths were dedicated to the maintenance of certain establishments. Up to 1810 the estate remained in the hands of the trustees appointed under the deed; but in that year they were accused of malversation, and, after protracted litigation, were dismissed in 1816. The Government then constituted itself a trustee, and assumed the management of the estate and the superintendence of the disbursements in conjunction with another trustee appointed by itself. In 1817, the estate was farmed out in *putnee*, that is, settled in perpetuity at fixed rates with the tenants. The amounts received from the tenants as consideration for the *putnee* settlement, with the arrears which had accumulated during litigation and the one-ninth share drawn by Government as trustee, were in 1835 devoted to the building and endowment of an institution at Hugli, comprising English and Oriental Departments. This appropriation of the trust funds was justified on the ground that the maintenance of an educational institution was a "pious use," and so within the testator's intentions.

This College was opened on the 1st August 1836, and within three days counted 1,200 pupils in the English and 300 in the Oriental Department; the proportion of Muhammadans to Hindus being 31 to 948 in the former, and 138 to 81 in the latter. It seems to have been left out of consideration that the interpretation placed on the declared intentions of the founder could only be applicable to Muhammadan education. This naturally was regarded as a grievance by the Muhammadan community.

In course of time large accumulations to the credit of the trust accrued and the subject attracted the attention of Government. The Government of India in 1872 desired that the whole subject of the application of the funds in promotion of Muhammadan education should be fully considered and plans matured for their disbursement more in consonance with the intentions of Muhammad Mohsin. The Government of Bengal put forward certain suggestions as to the utilisation of the funds. It proposed to reform the Hugli Madrasah, and to take upon itself the non-Musalman side of the Hugli College, hitherto entirely supported from the Mohsin Funds, but at the same time to accept from the funds a fair contribution for the Madrasah attached to the College and for special benefit to Muhammadan students studying in the College. As in the opinion of the Lieutenant-Governor (Sir George Campbell) it would be difficult to justify the devotion of provincial funds to special Muhammadan Education in the province generally, while the Mohsin endowment supplied a legitimate means of effecting the purpose in view, the Government of Bengal further expressed its intention to devote the money thus saved from the Hugli College to aid and extend Muhammadan education elsewhere. Proposals for the establishment of new Madrasahs at Dacca and other local centres in Eastern and Northern Bengal were then explained in detail ; but as the Mohsin funds were not adequate to enable Government to equip efficiently the new Madrasahs, the Lieutenant-Governor trusted that the Government of India would contribute to make up the difference.

In reply the Government of India wrote thus to the Government of Bengal :—"The general principles upon which the

Lieutenant-Governor desires to see these institutions administered and directed for the better promotion of high Muhammadan education appear to the Government of India to be sound......It is agreed, by common consent, that the intention of the British Government in supporting these institutions is to give to Muhammadans their full share of high-class intellectual training and of sound knowledge useful to them in life, combined but not clashing with that Oriental erudition which belongs to their race and country. And it is also agreed that in shaping our methods towards these ends we are bound to avoid, so far as may be possible, any unwelcome abandonment of the old ways of Muhammadan study, or any slight upon the classic learning of Muhammadan Asia. On the contrary the importance to Muhammadans of such studies is admitted, and their intrinsic value as instruments of literary training in this country is not under-rated.

"But the point of difficulty is also recognised by all to whom the subject is familiar. It lies in the problem of framing for Muhammadans a course of secular education, which is the only kind that can be given in Government institutions, upon the study of a literature which on so many sides of it is intimately connected with their religion and doctrinal tenets.

"His Excellency, nevertheless, believes that the problem thus presented is capable of solution, that a course of study can be laid down which shall maintain and encourage the cultivation of Arabic and Persian, of the history, literature, and philosophy which these languages convey, of their logical system, and of such parts of Muhammadan Law as deal with purely temporal interests, without compromising the Government to the support of any peculiar school of religious teaching." After referring with approval to the details of the proposals regarding the re-organisation of the Madrasahs, the Government of India continued with reference to the Hugli institution "The Lieutenant-Governor's proposition is to withdraw the greater part of the Mohsin Funds from the Hugli College, which has no particular local claim, and to use the money for encouraging Muhammadan education elsewhere, apportioning it according to need......His Excellency in Council approves the outlines of this proposal, and considers that some such arrangement would be consistent with the purposes of the Mohsin endowment, and generally advantageous to Muhammadan education. But, with regard to the employment of the Mohsin funds thus to be set free, His Excellency remarks that there are such valid objections to any separate system of denominational schools or colleges that the Government of India prefers not to move further in that direction, although there is no intention of disturbing what may already exist...... the high schools or colleges at Chittagong and Dacca, in the midst of a great Muhammadan population, might be thus reinforced both in the way of teaching Arabic and Persian more thoroughly and of generally cheapening education to Muhammadans by scholarships and the like. Or a portion of the Mohsin Funds might go toward increasing the public grants-in-aid of Muhammadan schools and colleges."

The details of any scheme which might be worked upon this design were left in the hands of the Bengal Government. As to the request for Imperial aid, the Government of India consented, chiefly in view of Sir George Campbell's scheme for encouraging Muhammadan education, to increase the regular provincial assignment by an annual additional grant of Rs. 50,000.

Madrasahs were accordingly established at Dacca, Chittagong and Rajshahi, scholarships were created for Muhammadan youths attending schools and colleges, and allotments were made from the Mohsin Fund to some of the Zilla schools for paying two-thirds of the fees of poor Muhammadan students and for appointing Persian teachers. These measures seem to have produced the desired effect, and perceptible improvement in Muhammadan education appears to have taken place during the next decade.

CHAPTER IV.

RECOMMENDATIONS OF THE EDUCATION COMMISSION.

The Education Commission, appointed by Lord Ripon in 1882, made an exhaustive inquiry into the subject, consulting all available reports and resolutions and examining veteran Muhammadan educationists as witnesses. After thoroughly threshing out the subject they formulated the following recommendations for the further encouragement of Muhammadan Education :—

(1) That the special encouragement of Muhammadan education be regarded as a legitimate charge on Local, Municipal, and on Provincial Funds;

(2) That indigenous Muhammadan schools be liberally encouraged to add purely secular subjects to their course of instruction ;

(3) That special standards for Muhammadan primary schools be prescribed ;

(4) That Hindustani be the principal medium for imparting instruction to Muhammadans in primary and middle schools, except in localities where the Muhammadan community desire that some other language be adopted ;

(5) That the official vernacular, in places where it is not Hindustani, be added as a voluntary subject to the curriculum of primary and middle schools for Muhammadans maintained from public funds, and that arithmetic and accounts be taught through the medium of the vernacular ;

(6) That in localities where Muhammadans form a fair proportion of the population, provision be made in middle and high schools maintained from public funds for imparting instruction in the Hindustani and Persian languages ;

(7) That higher English education for Muhammadans,

2

being the kind of education in which that community needs special help, be liberally encouraged ;

(8) That where necessary a graduated system of special scholarships for Muhammadans be established, to be awarded *(a)* in primary schools, and tenable in middle schools, *(b)* in middle schools, and tenable in high schools *(c)* on the result of the Matriculation and Fir. Arts Examinations, and tenable in Colleges ;

(9) That in all classes of schools maintained from public funds a certain proportion of free studentships be expressly reserved for Muhammadan students ;

(10) That in places where educational endowments for the benefit of Muhammadans exist, and are under the management of Government, the funds arising from such endowments be devoted to the advancement of education among Muhammadans exclusively ;

(11) That where Muhammadan endowments exist, and are under the management of private individuals or bodies, inducements by liberal grants-in-aid be offered to them to establish English teaching schools or colleges on the grant-in-aid system ;

(12) That, where necessary, normal schools or classes for the training of Muhammadan teachers be established ;

(13) That, wherever instruction is given in Muhammadan schools through the medium of Hindustani, endeavours be made to secure, as far as possible, Muhammadan teachers to give such instruction ;

(14) That Muhammadan inspecting officers be employed more largely than hitherto for the inspection of primary schools for Muhammadans ;

(15) That associations for the promotion of Muhammadan education be recognised and encouraged ;

(16) That in the annual reports on public instruction a special section be devoted to Muhammadan education ;

(17) That the attention of Local Governments be invited

to the question of the proportion in which patronage is distributed among educated Muhammadans and others.

In proposing these measures the Commission reviewed the general situation thus.—

"Apart from the social and historical conditions of the Muhammadan community in India, there are causes of a strictly educational character which heavily weigh it in the race of life. The teaching of the mosque must precede the lessons of the school. The one object of a young Hindu is to fit him for an official or professional career. But before the young Muhammadan is allowed to turn his thoughts to secular instruction he must commonly pass some years in going through a course of sacred learning. The Muhammadan boy, therefore, enters school later than the Hindu. In the second place, he very often leaves the school at an earlier age. The Muhammadan parent belonging to the better classes is usually poorer than the Hindu parent in a corresponding social position. He cannot afford to give his son so complete an education. In the third place, irrespective of his worldly means, the Muhammadan parent often chooses for his son while at school an education which will secure for him an honoured place among the learned of his community, rather than one which will command success in the modern professions or in official life. The years which the young Hindu gives to English and Mathematics in a public school the young Muhammadan devotes in a Madrasah to Arabic and the law and theology of Islam. When such an education is completed, it is to the vocation of a man of learning, rather than to the more profitable professions, that the thoughts of a promising Muhammadan youth naturally turn. The above are the three principal causes of an educational character which retard the prosperity of the Musalmans."

The Commission concluded their reports with the following observations :—

" Few of them, indeed, are of general application ; many

of them, we trust, will before long be rendered obsolete. Special encouragement to any class is itself an evil; and it will be a sore reproach to the Musalmans if the pride they have shown in other matters does not stir them up to a course of honourable activity, to a determination that whatever their backwardness in the past, they will not suffer themselves to be outstripped in the future, to a conviction that self-help and self-sacrifice are at once nobler principles of conduct and surer paths to worldly success than sectarian reserve or the hope of exceptional indulgence."

In reviewing the recommendations of the Commission, the Lieutenant-Governor of Bengal said, "The proposals for the support of special Muhammadan schools, and for the special encouragement of Muhammadan education in ordinary schools, are worthy of liberal consideration. Many of them are already in force in this province; the chief innovation being that for the creation of a special class of scholarships for Muhammadan students. To this, no doubt, objection may be made. The Lieutenant-Governor, however, thinks that if it can be shown that in any locality the number of Muhammadans who gain scholarships is not in due proportion to their numbers and position, a fair case will have been made out for exceptional, though he will also add temporary, treatment. The other recommendations under this head are conceived in a liberal spirit, and may be accepted, except in so far as they recognise the substitution of Hindustani for the Hindi vernacular. If by Hindustani be meant that language which, written in the Hindi or Nagri character, is the common speech alike of Muhammadan and Hindu in Behar, the Lieutenant-Governor has no objection to offer. But if the recommendation mean that the policy which has prevailed for some years, of conveying primary instruction to Muhammadans in Behar through Hindustani expressed in the Hindi character, is to be reversed, then the Lieutenant-Governor must very strongly dissent from the recommendation as being opposed to the true interests of the Muhammadans of Behar.

Finally the Lieutenant-Governor is not disposed to support the establishment of normal schools or classes for Muhammadan teachers exclusively. Little is gained by such separation."

The Marquis of Dufferin in a Resolution based on a memorial from the Central National Muhammadan Association observed, "It is only by frankly placing themselves in line with the Hindus, and taking full advantage of the Government system of high, and specially of English education, that the Muhammadans can hope fairly to hold their own in respect of the better description of the state appointments." His Excellency further remarked "The Governor-General in Council trusts that the Bengal Government will give effect to its views. There is no intention to reverse the decision of the Local Government in the matter of the adoption of Hindi as the Court language of Behar, and as the ordinary medium of instruction in the primary schools of that province. Where the Muhammadan population is strong and likely to attach special importance to Oriental teaching of a Muhammadan type, care should be taken to meet this want, with a view to making the schools popular and inducing the better classes to allow their children to push their studies eventually to a higher standard, specially in English. But equal care is necessary to prevent the absolute separation of the Muhammadan community from the rest of the population. It must be borne in mind that it is only by an acquaintance with the current vernacular that Muhammadans can hope to secure employment."

The Resolution directed "that in accordance with the recommendation of the Education Commission a special section in the annual reports on public instruction be devoted to Muhammadan education. These reports should be precise and detailed, and discuss the position and advancement of the Muhammadan community, not merely as a whole, but with reference to local variations, in order that the Government of India may be kept fully informed as to the state and progress of this important section of the community. For the attraction of Muhammadans to higher education, a liberal provision of scholarships is essential, and their wants must not be overlooked in the framing of any general scheme of scholarships for any province. Probably the appointment of special Muhammadan Inspecting officers to inspect not merely primary schools, but to enquire into Muhammadan education generally, would have a good effect in Bengal and other places where the Muhammadans are very backward. Such officers would bring the peculiar wants of their co-religionists more thoroughly to notice than can perhaps be expected from subordinate officers of a different faith. The action taken in those and other directions should be fully explained in the annual reports."

CHAPTER V.

APPOINTMENT OF MUHAMMADAN ASSISTANT INSPECTORS OF SCHOOLS.

Since then a section in the annual reports has always been devoted to Muhammadan education, special scholarships have been created for Muhammadans, of which a detailed account will be given later on, and two special Assistant Inspectors of schools have been appointed in Bengal. In making the proposal for the appointment of these Inspecting officers the Director of Public Instruction observed "What seems to be required is the presence in every circle of an educated Muhammadan, able and willing, to influence his co-religionists in favour of Western education and to watch over the interests of Muhammadan schools and pupils." The two Assistant Inspectors were appointed in January 1889. As the instructions issued to these officers are likely to prove interesting I shall quote some of them—"The object with which these appointments have been sanctioned is the improvement of

Muhammadan education generally in schools of every class. For this purpose the Assistant Inspector is required, in the first instance, to ascertain the special educational wants of Muhammadans in his circle, and to report them to the Inspector for any further orders of the Department or of Government that may be necessary ; and, in the next place, to endeavour to acquire influence with those in authority among his co-religionists, in order to induce them to accept such changes and reforms in the system or the subjects of education as may be pronounced to be salutary......The difficulties that beset Muhammadan education are of two kinds—one arising from their poverty and the other from their religious prejudices. Both alike operate to prevent Muhammadans from taking full advantage of the educational facilities that exist. The difficulties that arise from poverty are not, in the present state of finances, very easy to deal with. Still it is desirable to know of what exact nature they are, and what measures of relief would avail to remove or alleviate them. In places where, out of a large Muhammadan population, a sufficient proportion do not attend the local English school, the cause may be that the pupils are too poor to pay the fees, or that the school is too poor to maintain a Moulvi and give them the education they desire. A beginning of relief in this direction has now been made by the appropriation of a small sum from the Mohsin Fund for the purpose of paying a portion of the fees of Muhammadan pupils, or of maintaining a Moulvi in a few selected schools frequented by Muhammadans......The difficulties that arise from prejudice in favour of a particular mode and special subjects of instruction require different measures of treatment. In this class of cases the object will be gained, if at all, not so much by expenditure of money as by the exercise of influence. The Assistant Inspector should, therefore, endeavour to gain the confidence and secure the good will of the leading members of the Muhammadan community—on the one hand, of Mianjis, Maulvis, and all who are directly engaged in teaching ; on the other, of men of position and influence, whose views on matters of education determine the attitude of the community at large on such questions. It should be explained and insisted on that the Government has no desire to interfere with the religious beliefs of Muhammadans, or to limit their opportunities of religious instruction ; but only, while protecting their spiritual, to advance their material interests. The Government, in its regard for all classes of its subjects alike, cannot offer appointments or other public advantages to Muhammadans, merely because they are Muhammadans ; but it desires to give them increased facilities for education, so that on the one hand, they may be in a position to compete on equal terms for those positions of honour and emolument to which education is the only passport, and that on the other, they may not, in the general advance of education throughout the land, be left behind."

Shortly after these posts were created I was appointed to one of them. After taking charge I issued a demi-official letter to all educated and influential Muhammadan gentlemen in Eastern Bengal, where I was first posted, inviting suggestions, and I spent some time in observation and in the accumulation of facts. I then submitted a series of reports to the Department. I shall briefly give you an account of the state of Muhammadan education in Bengal as far as I have been able to ascertain the facts and of the measures taken for its improvement. You will find that during the past decade more has been done to encourage and extend Muhammadan education in Bengal than was done in half a century before that. This may be itself taken as a fair record of work. It may, however, appear to you that what has been hitherto done with regard to the organisation of schools and the modification of the course of studies does not amount to a great deal. It may also appear that the sum granted by Government by way of subsidising schools and aiding their scholars is smaller than might have been expected, and that the number of Muhammadan educational officers does not satisfy our ambition.

This result is chiefly due to the conservative ideas of our co-religionists in matters of education on the one hand and to financial pressure on the other. Those who have experience of such matters are aware that it is very difficult to persuade Musalmans, especially Moulvies and Mianjis engaged in educational work, to exchange their former modes of study for others more consonant with modern habits of thought, although they have already learnt "that the ancient paths are unprofitable to stand upon." Yet as will be shown later on perceptible progress has already been made. As for the amount of Government aid it must be remembered that in these evil days when frontier defence and frontier expenditure, famine and pestilence swallow up enormous amounts, expenditure has to be curtailed in every direction possible, and new grants cannot be freely given. Yet we must gratefully record the fact that important help has been given pecuniarily in the form of grants to schools and stipends to scholars. In connection with the paucity of appointments it should be borne in mind that the qualifications for Government service have gradually been so raised that the present minimum of literary instruction required to qualify for Government posts is greater than the previous maximum. Our Hindu fellow-countrymen have not only acquired the requisite educational qualifications but they have also succeeded in gaining recognition. There is no denying the fact that for one Muhammadan qualified candidate for educational appointments ten equally qualified Hindus come forward as his rivals, and naturally the majority of appointments go to them. Officials cannot show any favour, however just, to a particular community without being pilloried in the public Press. Again family influence is all in favour of Hindus. Hindu officers are predominant in every department of Government service; and their relatives have naturally a better chance of securing vacant posts than Musalmans. European Officials who have the gift of such posts naturally prefer connections of Government servants to strangers. It is but natural that Hindu officers should favour their co-religionists. I doubt whether

2 A

Musalmans would do otherwise were they in a similar position. The misfortune of the Musalmans is that they did not receive English education early enough.

These are some of the adverse circumstances that stand in the way of Muhammadan candidates for Government service. Notwithstanding these difficulties, however, in the Education Department more Muhammadans have obtained responsible posts during the last five years than during the previous twenty-five.

CHAPTER VI.

MAKTABS.

I shall consider the subject of Muhammadan education under three heads, viz. Primary, Secondary and Higher education. I shall describe first the condition in which I found these on my appointment, secondly what has been done during the last decade, and thirdly what yet remains to be done. In my tours in various districts of Eastern Bengal I found many Muhammadan institutions almost all of which go by the common name of Maktab. On examination they were found to differ greatly in their characteristics and course of studies. These Maktabs may be sub-divided into four classes, viz. the Koran schools, the pure or Urdu Maktabs, the mixed or Bengali Maktabs and the Madrasahs. The Koran schools teach nothing but Arabic spelling and recitation of the verses of the Koran. These cannot be called educational institutions, for, if the Koran reading constitutes education, about 90 per cent, if not more, of the Musalmans are educated. Almost every Musalman knows how to recite at least some verses of the Koran. Every well-to-do Musalman in Lower Bengal engages a Mianji to teach the Koran to his children and the Mianji invites the neighbouring poor Muhammadans to place their children under his tuition. Thus there are numerous Koran schools, many of which are not included in our educational returns. In most cases the Mianjis are illiterate men who are acquainted only with the Arabic alphabet and some of them have been heard to boast that they learnt to recite the Koran without even that knowledge. As some of the Mianjis protract their course of instruction to an unnecessary length of time, they do great harm to their pupils. Year after year I have had occasion to visit some of these schools and to enquire of the progress of the pupils. Every time I learnt that the Koran was not yet finished. As finishing the Koran means the loss of the teacher's occupation if there is no younger son in the family to be taught, the teacher purposely protracts his instruction. It is very desirable that the educated Musalmans of Bengal should impress upon their un-enlightened and illiterate co-religionists that there are great disadvantages in entrusting the early education of their children to illiterate Mianjis.

These Koran schools are of no educational value. I pointed out in my report to Government that injustice is done to Muhammadans by returning the Koran schools as edcational institutions and counting their pupils as Muhammadan boys under instruction. The inclusion of such institutions in the educational statistics makes the high percentage of Muhammadan pupils shown in the annual reports somewhat misleading. Although the Koran schools have not been excluded from the educational returns on the ground that they are included in the returns under a special order of the Government of India, and cannot be excluded till that order is rescinded, their educational utility being repeatedly called in question, they are now rated at their true worth, and the rise or fall in their pupils is no longer supposed to signify the advancement or retrogression of Muhammadan education.

The pure Maktabs teach the Urdu and Persian languages in addition to the Koran. The method of teaching is old-fashioned and not calculated to develop the intellectual faculties of the boys. As soon as Urdu spelling has been learnt the tenets of Islam are taught from a comprehensive book on the subject named *Miftahul Jannat.* The boys have to learn at the age of nine or ten detailed rules regarding *Ghusl,* (bath), *Haiz* (menstruation) and *Nefas* (child birth). Do boys derive any benefit by learning such subjects at such an early age? The answer, I am afraid, will have to be given in the negative. On the contrary these topics suggest to their young minds ideas which they should be ignorant of, till they attain to manhood. In the interest of our young men careful attention should be paid by educated Musalmans to the demoralising tendency of this method of instruction. For, this is, not unlikely, the cause of the immoral tendencies and impure ideas which some boys seem to imbibe even at an early age. As far as I know there is hardly any book on the tenets of Islam that may be safely placed in the hands of young boys. This is a keenly-felt want which should be at once supplied by one of our learned Ulamas. A short chapter on the life of our holy Prophet and the rise of Islam, and a few chapters on the fundamental principles of Islam and on the tenets and rules regarding ablution, prayer and kindred subjects, would form an admirable text-book. I am not in favour of teaching select portions of a comprehensive work. The omission of particular portions of a book only rouses the curiosity of an intelligent boy, who reads them on his own account. It is not at all desirable that young boys should be taught such rules as are likely to suggest impure ideas to their young minds. Instruction on such topics should be postponed to a later stage of life.

As regards Persian, the method of teaching is equally objectionable. As soon as a boy finishes the Persian spelling book he is made to learn, of course by rote, "*Ke hustam asiri kamande hawa*". A boy of eight or nine can scarcely understand what "*kamande hawa*" is and how a man is made its captive. Thus the manner of teaching Urdu and Persian in the Maktabs, far from developing the intelligence of our boys, serves only to cramp and dwarf it.

I frequently point out to the Mianjis, when I visit their Maktabs, the objectionable features of their teaching and draw their attention particularly to the fact that while their average pupils after years of study fail to write letters or keep accounts correctly, the pupils of the Patshalas after going through the second and third Bengali primers in about two years are able to write letters and keep accounts satisfactorily. I have succeeded in introducing into several of these institutions such Urdu and Persian primers as have been published by the Anjumani Hemayet Islam, Lahore.

These Maktabs if properly organised and taught are likely to prove useful institutions for the primary education of Muhammadan boys. I represented this to the Department and proposed that the course of studies for such Maktabs should be officially prescribed and that they should be assisted by grants-in-aid. This meant of course that Urdu also should be recognised as a language for Primary education among the Musalmans of Bengal. The Director of Public Instruction issued a circular on the subject inviting suggestions from the educational officers. One of the Inspectors strongly objected to this on the ground that Urdu is not the mother-tongue of the Musalmans of Bengal, nor is it the court-language of the province. In his opinion Urdu is not at all necessary for the lower class of Musalmans and they should not be encouraged to ape at the accomplishments of the gentry. Another Inspector reported that the Musalmans in his division do not in the least care for Urdu. In reply to the first, I pointed out the necessity of Urdu on religious grounds and to the second it was shown that the majority of the Musalmans inhabiting the districts referred to are Musalmans by conversion and not by descent. The proposal was, however, modified. It is not at all desirable to create anywhere a demand for Urdu ; but in places where there is a demand it should be supplied. After further discussion of the subject it was decided that for the present Urdu should be recognised only for the Maktabs of Calcutta and efforts should be made to convert the pure Maktabs elsewhere into mixed Maktabs. Subjects of Urdu text-books for the Calcutta Maktabs have already been prescribed and some of them receive grants-in-aid. But so opposed are the Mianjis to any official interference with what they teach and so firmly wedded are they to their ancient ways that though they are required to teach all the subjects through the medium of Urdu not even one-tenth of the Maktabs in Calcutta have adopted the standards and books prescribed by the Department.

The mixed Maktabs are very useful institutions. The Departmental standards in Bengali are taught in them in addition to the Koran, Urdu and Persian. I am of opinion that these ought to be the only true Primary schools for the Musalmans of Bengal. The more I study the subject the more I am convinced that the only satisfactory solution of the question is a combination of religious and secular education —of the education at present given in the Maktabs, with that given in the Patshalas. I shall show later on, while treating of the necessity of creating a vernacular literature for the Musalmans of Bengal, how Islam is ceasing to have any hold on those who are being educated in the ordinary Primary schools (Patshalas) of this country. If once boys be thoroughly well-grounded in the principles of Islam, their faith is not likely to be easily shaken by the education they may afterwards receive in institutions meant for the higher education of all classes. You are aware that the material interests of those who study in pure Maktabs have been suffering. The Musalmans of Bengal should do their best to persuade the teachers of the Maktabs to adopt the vernacular standards and to teach them properly. This will obviate the necessity of giving Muhammadan boys religious education at home before they join the public schools. They will no longer begin their secular education, as they at present do, at an age later than that of Hindu boys and thus they will not be handicapped in their progress. The Musalmans should also try their best to induce Government to aid these institutions by grants on a liberal scale. The argument may be used with regard to Muhammadan boys, which was once used with regard to European children, that they should be required to attend the ordinary schools of the country. This argument could not be maintained in face of the strong objection that European parents had to sending their children to schools where they would receive no religious instruction and where the whole atmosphere would be non-Christian. The principle of making special provision for European children was thus established. If proper representations regarding this subject were made to Government by Muhammadans, they would likely be taken into favourable consideration. No attempt should, however, be made to have separate Middle or High schools for Musalmans. It is only Primary schools which should be separately organised and supported. I am afraid the remarks of the Director in 1872 regarding the inducements necessary for the spread of Muhammadan Education are still valid even after more than a quarter of a century. They still require the inducements held out sixty-five years ago to the whole community. Unless the strong inducements in general vogue at that time are held out to Musalmans now there is not much chance of seeing the Mianjis reforming their Maktabs in the desired direction. It is not possible to induce Government to start Government Maktabs as was suggested by Sir William Hunter. He wrote thus "The grant-in-aid rules will not reach a population averse to our system of instruction. But fifty cheap schools with low-paid Musalman teachers would in a single generation change the popular tone of Eastern Bengal. They would gradually attract not merely the Musalman peasant youths, but also the Musalman teachers who now earn a precarious livelihood on their own account." I wish this suggestion had been acted upon. Had this been done the state of Muhammadan Education in Bengal would have been totally different from what it is now. The times have greatly changed, and suggestions like the one made by Sir William cannot be reasonably made now. The efforts of Musalmans should, therefore, be directed towards securing for the Maktabs grants-in-aid on a liberal scale. In this connection the Director of Public Instruction said in his Report for the year 1889-90. "Payment by rewards may suit advanced races, but among a backward people like the Muhammadans it can never flourish. The Mianjis of the Maktabs are generally men with very few attainments; and whilst immediate inducements in the shape of fixed monthly stipends offered for a reasonable time, would secure the services of competent teachers, or bring the old ones round to learn and adopt the new mode of teaching, mere promised remuneration like those of the reward system would have no influence upon them." The stipendiary system is essential for the reorganisation and improvement of the Maktabs. The Government may make an allotment for the purpose from the Primary Fund and may direct the District Boards and Municipalities to grant stipends to Maktabs teaching the Departmental standards in Bengali, curtailing proportionately the allotment for reward. If this be done the Musalmans will no longer have any ground for complaining, as some of them are heard to complain "that the funds which are levied impartially from all classes for State Education are expended on a system exclusively adapted to the Hindus."

In connection with the reorganisation of the Maktabs the Musalmans of Orissa have acted very wisely. This province was conquered by the Musalmans not long before the extinction of their empire. Consequently few of the inhabitants were real converts to Islam. The Muhammadan inhabitants of Orissa are almost all Musalmans by descent and their mother-tongue is Urdu. There are few, if any, Muhammadan agriculturists. In this respect there is a great difference between Bengal and Orissa. The Musalmans in Orissa number only about 2·3 per cent of the total population. They are the descendants of the military men who conquered the province. Some of them are now landed proprietors, others are members of various professions. On the occasion of my first visit to Orissa prominent Musalmans represented to me that the education of their children was being entirely neglected as there was no properly organised Urdu school. Although Dr. Martin, the then Director of Public Instruction, was strongly opposed to the recognition of Urdu as the language of primary education for the Musalmans of Bengal (it was he who did not wish to see the peasants "aping at the accomplishments of the gentry") he readily consented to recognise Urdu as the language through which primary education should be given to the Musalmans of Orissa, on the ground that it was their mother-tongue. He was willing to sanction an allotment for the Urdu schools in Orissa. At that time I visited Balasore and held a meeting of Musalmans at which this subject was discussed. I pointed out to them that they were not likely to gain anything at least from a wordly point of view, by giving their children secular education through the medium of Urdu while Uriya is the language of the Courts in Orissa. After a good deal of discussion, common sense prevailed and it was decided that among the Musalmans of Orissa the language of the secular primary schools should be Uriya. Accordingly in the Madrasah at Balasore which has been raised to the status of a Middle English school, instruction is given in Uriya. Of course there is an Oriental Department which teaches Urdu and Persian. Uriya has already been introduced into some of the Maktabs in Orissa and they have received grants. The good example set by the Musalmans of Orissa, who, although they were on the point of receiving what they had so long desired, adopted a different platform at the dictates of common sense, is well worth imitation by their co-religionists in Bengal, and I hope before long all the Maktabs in Bengal will adopt Bengali as the teaching language. The educated Musalmans of Bengal should exert their influence to this end.

As I have never officially visited Behar I have no practical knowledge of the state of Muhammadan education

3

there. Behar was under my colleague, the other special Muhammadan Assistant Inspector. As far as I have been able to gather from educational statistics it seems that the Musalmans of Behar are not behind their neighbours, the Hindus, in education. They are decidedly more advanced than Musalmans in Bengal. Probably the reason of this is the fact that Urdu was the court language and had been the medium of primary education in Behar, for a long time.

Before the conclusion of my remarks on Primary education, a few words regarding the subjects and text-books to be taught in the Maktabs will not be out of place. In consideration of the dual character of these institutions books in Urdu and Persian and in Bengali will have to be prescribed. Government is not likely either to prescribe Urdu and Persian text-books for the Maktabs or to test the progress of the pupils in these subjects. For, this will require a separate agency which Government is not likely to maintain. The educated Musalmans of Bengal should bestir themselves in this matter. They should bring pressure to bear upon the Mianjis and Maulavis to remedy the defects in the method of teaching Urdu and Persian. For religious education a small compendium in Urdu of the kind indicated above should be selected or prepared. As for Urdu and Persian literature a graduated series of readers suited to the capacity of the various classes of boys and likely to develop their intellectual faculties should be taught. It is very desirable that the Urdu and Persian books taught in the Maktabs should be the same as those taught in the lower classes of the Madrasahs, so that a boy, after completing his Maktab course, may join a higher class of the Madrasah if he desires to become an Oriental scholar. As for testing the progress in Urdu and Persian, is it not possible for the educated Musalmans of every district to create an agency for the purpose after the model of Inspectors appointed by Christian Societies for inspecting their mission schools? They may engage some Maulavis, whose number is legion, to inspect and examine the Maktabs. The Departmental officers, I have no doubt, will gladly help them.

As for the Bengali course of studies, what is prescribed by the Education Department should be bodily adopted, so that boys on completing their Maktab course may pass into the middle schools. The introduction of English primers will add to the utility and popularity of Maktabs. If the Mianji happens to know a little English, he should teach this also. Boys so taught will not have to join the lowest class of an English school, by which they lose some years. I am glad that a few Maktabs in East Bengal have already, at my suggestion, added a little English to the course.

CHAPTER VII.

SYSTEM OF PRIMARY EDUCATION.

Primary education is of greater moment than secondary education, and in India its importance is higher than elsewhere. India is remarkable for the numerical insignificance of the middle and upper classes. A large majority of the population are devoted to the cultivation of Mother-Earth ; "about seven-tenths directly, nine-tenths altogether are supported by agriculture." The system of Primary education, therefore, needs very careful attention.

As the Maktabs will have to teach the vernacular course prescribed for the Patshalas and as a large number of Muhammadan boys, specially in places where Musalmans by conversion preponderate and where Maktabs are few and far between, will have to attend the ordinary primary schools, the Musalmans should not abstain from taking part in the discussion that is going on regarding the system of primary education in Bengal. It has been proposed to replace some of the literary subjects at present taught by others of a more technical and scientific character, and an agitation is going on regarding this matter. It appears to me that both parties in this discussion entertain extreme views from altogether different standpoints. Perhaps a compromise will best suit the real requirements of the people.

My attention was accidentally drawn to this subject some years ago. While visiting a school in the district of Backergunge, I found its financial condition very far from what it should have been. I was urging upon the people, who met me after the inspection was over, the necessity of liberally supporting the school, when I heard one man whispering to another that he would give "*Harilut*" on the day the school ceased to exist. As these words were not meant for my ears I did not take any notice of them at that time. When the people were gone I enquired of the local Inspector of Police, who came to see me, why the residents of the place seemed disgusted with the school. What he said convinced me that the people had reason to be dissatisfied with the school and perhaps the man who whispered, as one of the greatest sufferers, would have actually expressed his joy at the abolition of the school by giving a *Harilut*. The place was largely inhabited by petty shop-keepers, who required the assistance of their boys in selling goods and in keeping accounts. But no sooner were the boys sent to the school than they gave themselves airs and looked down upon shop-keeping as unworthy of those who could read. This incident led me to enquire into the subject and from what I have since seen and heard I have reason to believe that the existence of a Patshala in their neighbourhood has been a source of trouble to many a peasant family. Even against his will a peasant feels bound to send his son to the village Patshala either through the persuasion of the Guru or the importunity of the boy who wants to join the other boys of the village at school. Once the boy sets his foot within the hallowed precincts of the school, he becomes a totally different creature. After his acquaintance with the alphabet even his peasant name seems unbecoming to his position as a student and he does not hesitate to change it. In going through the Patshala records it is found not unfrequently that a boy whose name in the register of the last class was Mandal has in the register of the next class become Bisvash—a term which is supposed to signify some literary attainments. His parents not only lose his assistance in tending cattle and cultivating fields but are obliged to supply him with good clothes, good shoes and a good umbrella, at a cost far beyond their means. After acquiring a smattering of Bengali, for, either his means or his intelligence does not allow him to proceed further, he becomes a burden upon his family. He hates to earn his livelihood by manual labour, and knows nothing else by which he can make a living. Thus has many a peasant suffered from the present system of primary education in Bengal. It seems very desirable that some such system of technical Education as is contemplated by the authorities should be introduced. I would not, however, be satisfied with giving mere theoretical knowledge of technical or scientific subjects. I would have a field attached to every primary school, intended for the labouring classes, so that when the science of agriculture is taught the Guru may practically illustrate what he teaches. My object is not only to teach boys how to handle a plough or till the ground, but also to remove the false impression that agriculture is derogatory to a Guru and his pupils. It is, however, very necessary that the utility of the rotation of crops, the use and utility of manure and such important subjects should be properly illustrated. All the scientific and technical subjects included in the curriculum of the Patshalas should be thus practically taught. Then, and not till then, will the children of the labouring classes really benefit by the education they receive. They will then regard what they may learn of literary subjects as an accomplishment worth acquiring for its own sake and not as a ladder by which they may rise in social status or a means of gaining bread. Then they will, after completing their Patshala course of studies, return to the fields or to other spheres of business and look upon manual labour as being as decent a means of gaining a livelihood as quill-driving.

Had the Primary schools in Bengal been attended, as is the case in the Central Provinces and in some other parts of India, mostly by the children of artisans, labourers and agriculturists, the system of primary education I have indicated above would have been the only system required. But Primary schools in Bengal are largely attended by the children of middle class people. To many of these boys Primary education is not, as to agriculturists, the only education they will ever have, but only the first stage of a long course of education to be completed in higher institutions. Primary schools are to them merely preparatory classes for the middle and high schools. They pass from the Primary to the Middle schools and thence to the high schools and colleges. In the Primary schools they are thoroughly grounded in subjects like Arithmetic, Geometry and Geography, taught in the vernacular language. By their proficiency in these subjects they often achieve brilliant success in their University career. Instances are not wanting of students who had previously passed the Primary and Middle Scholarship examinations, heading the list of successful candidates in the University examinations.

The question now arises whether the boys of the middle class will take to the system of Primary education indicated above. The answer, I am afraid, will have to be given in the negative. In this conservative and caste-ridden country, where manual labour has been regarded as degrading from time out of mind, people do not readily take to such innovations, however advantageous they may be. Perhaps it is more difficult to make a Brahman or a Kayastha into a blacksmith or a potter than to make him a Musalman or a Christian. Though among the Musalmans there is no hereditary caste by profession there is among them something akin to it in social rank and position. The son of a Zemindar or a Maulavi will be the last man, unless he starves, to adopt the profession of a potter or basket-maker.

The middle class in Bengal have been quill-drivers from time immemorial, and although western education is slowly but surely levelling down caste and social distinctions, it will be long before manual labour will cease to be regarded as something beneath the rank of the middle class. Few of the Mianjis of our Maktabs are likely to learn and teach clay-modelling and basket-making, just as they were long opposed even to the present system of education.

If a system of Primary education suited only to the requirements of the labouring classes were insisted upon, the result perhaps would be that most of the technical subjects would be entirely neglected or the Primary schools would be deserted by a large number of their pupils. Even if some boys of this class attend the Primary schools and have to make clay figures, paper kites, and bamboo baskets, they are likely to look upon these as mere amusements and not as a means of earning an independent living. Some of the middle class boys now attending Primary schools, who may be able to pay for higher education, will join higher schools, while others, probably, will receive no education at all.

To meet the needs of both classes of students it seems desirable that either there should be two systems of Primary education or that middle schools should be kept altogether separate from primary schools so that boys of the middle class may receive Primary education in the middle schools. To have two systems of Primary education in the same country and under the same government may look like an anomaly. But in a country of heterogenous populations among whom there exist stringent regulations of society, such anomalies have to be reckoned upon. It does not seem possible to blend the two systems together. For one should be more technical and less literary and the other more literary and less technical. The attempt to blend the two is likely to prove a failure and to frustrate both objects. If it is the intention of Government to withdraw gradually from higher education, and to spend the major portion of the educational grant on Primary education the two classes of schools might be maintained side by side. If, however, this is not possible, and Government decides to help only those who cannot help themselves, the people of the country will have to arrange for the Primary education of their children, as they are gradually providing higher education on their own account. In that case Government will have to be asked to recognise the system and to test the progress of the boys by its officers through Departmental examinations.

As for the middle schools, perhaps 90 per cent of their boys come from the respectable classes. It is desirable that this should be so. The education of the children of the labouring classes should, as a rule, end in the highest class of the Primary school. By studying up to that standard they are likely to learn all that they need to know. It does not seem advisable to give them an education befitting only a higher status of society or Government service which they cannot hope to attain. Exceptionally intelligent boys, however, will push their studies further either by gaining scholarships or by other means. It is desirable, therefore, to keep Primary schools distinct from middle schools and to restrict agricultural and manual subjects to the former. The literary side should predominate in the middle schools and only such scientific subjects should be introduced into them as will be of use in after life as a means of earning an independent living. The present course of studies for middle schools requires modification so as to admit of the introduction of useful scientific and technical (not manual) subjects.

Mr. F. W. Thomas, scholar of Trinity College, Cambridge, in his *Le Bas* Prize essay on the "History and Prospects of British education in India" has assailed the present system of education. According to him "it is not high education that India needs; it is practical scientific education." "What is most desiderated is new knowledge applied to every kind of production." "Let knowledge be introduced in such a way" says he "as to give a practical test of its value by improving arts and manufactures and increasing man's actual power over nature for the production of wealth. We are far from neglecting the desirability of general culture. But this has a spontaneous tendency to grow up wherever needed. On no ground does it appear to be the great desideratum for India at this moment. It is to the spread of practical knowledge that we have chiefly to look not only for the advance in material prosperity which is so greatly needed, but also for the breaking down of prejudice and encouragement of fellow-feeling between men." There is no doubt that there is a great deal of truth in these remarks. No one can deny that India urgently requires scientific education. The wealth of the country in gold, iron, coal and other metals has as yet only been tapped. Nearly every commercial or manufacturing enterprise which has sprung up in the country has been introduced and managed solely by Europeans. Who with even a grain of sense will deny that such a deplorable state of things should be remedied as soon as possible? There can be no two opinions regarding the utility and urgent necessity of scientific and technical education. It should by all means be introduced into the country, and until sufficient advance is made in this direction more attention and more funds should be devoted to its furtherance. But is it desirable to desert literary and high education entirely? Is it true that the people without assistance from Government will be able to provide themselves with literary education? Have the civilized and advanced nations of Europe neglected literary education? Do the Government in those countries refrain from contributing to literary education? Are not literary men so much required for the prosperity and civilisation of a nation as scientific men? Have not literary men (poets and prose writers, philosophers and logicians) in every age and clime contributed greatly to the progress and prosperity which have made their nations what they are? These are questions which should be answered only after deep study and much deliberation. As I have not the necessary preparation and as I have, perhaps, already digressed from my legitimate subject, I shall leave these ques-

3 A

tions unanswered. As, however, any particular system of education that may be adopted is as likely to affect Musalmans as others, I have thought it not improper to put these questions to an assembly in which the educated Musalmans from different parts of India are present. The subject, I need scarcely say, ought to engage the careful attention of all educated Indians.

As Madrasahs (which I have called one kind of Maktabs) are properly speaking institutions for high education of Musalmans, I shall deal with them when I treat of higher education.

CHAPTER VIII.

SECONDARY EDUCATION.

I have already said much of what I had to say regarding secondary education. I use the term secondary education to cover training up to the Middle Vernacular and the Middle English standards. More than half the course of the secondary schools is taught in the primary schools. Boys coming from primary schools complete the secondary course in two years. As it has been proposed to introduce two separate courses, one literary and the other technical, into Entrance schools, it might be advisable to introduce two separate courses into middle schools.

As regards the progress of Muhammadans in secondary or middle education, I must admit that it is still far from what it should be, although a perceptible advance has been made during the decade under review. In 1889-90 only 418 Muhammadan candidates passed the Middle scholarship examination, whereas last year 728 Muhammadans where successful at this examination. The percentage of Musalmans in the total of successful candidates in these examinations was about 10·5 in

1889-90, while last year it rose to about 13·0. Thus it will be seen that some progress has been made when the present condition of Muhammadan boys under secondary education is compared with their condition ten years ago. But it is still far from satisfactory when compared with the total number of successful candidates.

The desirability of the recognition of Urdu as an optional subject for Muhammadan students in middle schools was strongly urged upon the Government, specially by the Musalmans of Orissa. The Director of Public Instruction in submitting a report on the subject to Government observed "It seems to me essential that Muhammadans, whether in Orissa or in Bengal, should be familiar with the vernacular of the province in which they live—Uriya or Bengali respectively—and therefore that they should continue to learn history and the other subjects of substantive instruction through the ordinary vernacular text-books along with their Hindu class-fellows. To do otherwise would be to split the school into two independent sections. But I see no objection to allowing Muhammadans, in any school which can provide the requisite means of instruction, to learn Urdu while the Hindu students are learning Bengali or Uriya. Then at the Middle Scholarship Examination Muhammadan boys would be required to answer the history and other papers in Bengali or in Uriya, as the case might be, but for the language proper they would take up Urdu instead of the ordinary Vernacular. I believe that this concession would be very highly valued by Muhammadans throughout Bengal and Orissa, even if they did not very largely take advantage of it. Whether they did so or not would depend partly upon the strength of their desire to learn Urdu instead of, or rather in addition to, the ordinary vernacular of the province, and partly by their ability to provide Urdu teacher in the local school. Where they were both desirous of appointing and able to appoint a separate teacher of Urdu, the increased cost of establishment would entitle them to apply for a larger grant-in-aid."

Sir Alfred Croft very truly said that the concession would be highly valued by Muhammadans even if they did not very largely take advantage of it. Few schools have appointed teachers of Urdu, and not even half a dozen Muhammadan boys in Bengal and Orissa have taken up Urdu for the Middle scholarship examination. It is not at all desirable that they should do so. Unless they know Bengali or Uriya well, it is not possible for them to be able to answer properly papers in history, geography and science, and to pass examinations. Nor can they be sufficiently well-grounded in Bengali or Uriya unless they study the language properly. Taking up Urdu by the Muhammadan students of Middle schools would be just like taking up French or German as the language for the Matriculation while papers in the other subjects were to be answered in English. Those boys who want to pass the middle scholarship examination should not take up Urdu instead of the vernacular of the Province. There, however, can be no objection to their studying it as an additional subject. The Maulavis who have been appointed in some Middle schools at my instance, are meant not so much to teach Urdu as to attract Muhammadan boys to the school. The presence of even one Muhammadan teacher in a school inspires confidence among the local Musalmans, many of whom do not hesitate to send their children to the school in the hope that their morals and manners, to which Musalmans attach great importance, will be properly looked after. The Maulavis in the Middle schools have been instructed to teach Urdu out of school hours and as an additional subject.

Text-Books.—The next important question is that ofBengali text-books. One of the reasons, that are said to have deterred Musalmans from sending their children to ordinary schools, is the use in them of books whose tone is hostile or scornful to the Muhammadan community or to Islam and of books full of Hindu ideas and sentiments. On this subject I submitted a report to the Director of Public Instruction pointing out that Bengali books on literature used in the primary and middle schools being composed by Hindus, are naturally full of Hindu ideas and sentiments, of illustrations from Hindu mythology and history, and of quotations from the Hindu Shastras. The study of these books, it is said, makes Muhammadan boys forget the ideas of their own community. As soon as a Muhammadan boy enters a school he has to commit to memory such names as Ram, Sham, Jadab and Madhab, while he has hardly any occasion to pronounce names like Zaid, Amar, Ahmad and Muhammad. Hindu mythological names such as Lakshmi, Sarasvathi, Kali and Durga, names of Hindu reformers like Chaitanya, Gautama, Ramanuja and Ramananda are well known to Muhammadan pupils attending vernacular schools, while the names even of the four companions of their holy Prophet are unknown to them. Their ideal male character is Ram or Judhishthir while they do not seem to have heard of such characters as Khalid-Ibn-Walid or Harunar Rashid. They quote Sabitri and Sita as models of chastity while they do not know who Mariam and Fatima were. They can recite with ease passages from Sitar Banabash and Megnadbadh but are totally ignorant of works like Tuwarikhul Khulafa or Futuhushsham. Thus the Muhammadan boys, it is said, become in a manner Hinduised—Hindu in their thoughts and expressions and to some extent in their manners and behaviour. Instances of these influences working great changes in some of the Musalmans, are not wanting; some of them have gone even to the length of calling their children by Hindu names.

Again in some of the Bengali books on literature and history composed by Hindus, the language used with regard to some of the Muhammadan kings and their courtiers, is very distasteful to Musalmans. Some of the Hindu writers in speaking of Muhammadan heroes have made use of opprobrious terms and unmannerly expressions such as দুরন্ত, দুর্বৃত্ত, দুর্দান্ত, দুরাত্মা. পাষণ্ড, পামর which should never have found a place in books intended to be used in schools open to all communities. The fact that Muhammadan boys reading these

Bengali books imbibe unpalatable ideas with regard to their religion and nationality was shown to constitute a real grievance. It was also pointed out that Muhammadans have no racial prejudice against Hindu authors, for, they raise no objection to books on Bengali Grammar, Mathematics, and Science composed by Hindu authors. It was proposed that passages and expressions objectionable to Muhammadans be expunged from all Bengali school books on literature and history, that alternative text-books in Bengali literature having nothing sectarian in them, or books composed by Muhammadans, be prescribed for Muhammadan pupils. It was also suggested that subventions be granted for good translations into Bengali from standard works in Persian, Arabic and other languages, and also for original studies, as was indeed directed by the Government of Lord Mayo and reiterated in the Resolution of the Government of India dated the 13th June 1873.

In reply to my representation, Sir Alfred Croft, the Director of Public Instruction, wrote "I fully recognise the drawback pointed out in the Assistant Inspector's letter; and I hope that with the extended adoption of Urdu for Bengali literature by Muhammadan candidates at the Middle scholarship examination the objection will disappear. I may add that I am not aware of any Bengali book in use in schools in which opprobrious terms are used of Muhammadans as a class, or of leading men of that religion. I accordingly request that the Assistant Inspector may be asked to point out particular instances, so that the attention of the Central Text-book Committee may be drawn to the matter. That body commonly exercises the greatest care in removing from the authorised list any text-books which contain expressions calculated to offend either Hindus, Muhammadans or others. No objection can, however, be taken to the use of condemnatory epithets in case of those persons, whether Muhammadan or other, whom the verdict of History has judged worthy of condemnation."

On receipt of this reply I wrote to several persons, specially to those who had drawn my attention to the subject, requesting them to point out the objectionable passages. I regret to have to say that only one gentleman favoured me with a reply. I have no time to look through all the Bengali text-books, and, moreover, I am not a Bengali scholar. I, however, read some of the books and pointed out some of the passages which, I believe, have been removed. If Muhammadans who know Bengali do not care to come forward, when asked to substantiate grievances, it is surely desirable that they should not trouble the authorities with their objections. I am a member of the Central Text-Book Committee and so are my friends, Maulavi Delawar Hosain Ahmad Khan Bahadur and Doctor Zahir Uddin Ahmad Khan Saheb. There is no doubt that the Committee, specially its impartial and conscientious President, Mr Justice Banerjee, exercise great discretion in removing expressions which are calculated to offend any particular community. But what may appear objectionable to an orthodox Muhammadan may not appear so to a Hindu. Unless, therefore, the objectionable passages are pointed out it is useless to cry for their removal. As for the suggestion to prescribe alternative text-books for Muhammadan boys, the difficulty is where the books are to come from. Musalman Bengali Literature has not yet a Syad Ahmad or a Hali, a Nazir Ahmad, or a Shibli, to enrich it. I am not aware of even one Bengali poem or prose work, written by a Muhammadan that may be prescribed for the Middle scholarship examination. It is very desirable that Muhammadans should bestir themselves in this matter without further delay. The Government seems to have been misinformed on the subject. In the Resolution passed by the Government of Lord Northbrook, it was said "One measure to which the Resolution of 1871 particularly adverted was the development of a vernacular literature for Muhammadans. His Excellency in Council would be slow to believe that such a literature still needed creation." If Bengali (and not Urdu) is meant the condition that His Excellency was not willing to believe is only too true. Even now, after the lapse of about a quarter of a century since that Resolution was penned, a Musalman Bengali literature needs creation. I hope the subject will engage the attention of the educated Musalmans of Bengal.

Scholarships.—One other important matter in connection with Secondary education is the award of scholarships. I have already told you in summarising the Reports and Resolutions of Government regarding Muhammadan education, that in reviewing the recommendations of the Education Commission the Government of Bengal remarked "that if it could be shown that in any locality the Muhammadans who gained scholarships are not in due proportion to their number and position, a fair case would be made out for exceptional, although temporary, treatment." Subsequently the Director of Public Instruction was called upon to inform the Government what proportion of the Primary and Middle scholarships had been obtained by Muhammadans and whether he considered the result to be in any instance so exceptional as to call for special remedial measures. After some correspondence the matter seems to have been dropped. On my appointment as Assistant Inspector, I again raised the question and showed by facts and figures how in several districts Muhammadans were not able to hold their own with the Hindus in competing for scholarships and failed to gain them in due proportion to their number and position. After years of correspondence on the subject, it has been at last decided to reserve for successful Muhammadan candidates a certain proportion of the existing scholarships in districts where Muhammadans preponderate and fail to gain scholarships in proportion to their number. This is, no doubt, a very important concession, but Muhammadans are not likely to be able to take full advantage of it till they enter schools at an earlier age. For, when a candidate has passed a certain age he is debarred from getting scholarships, even if he compete for them, on account of having passed the prescribed age limit. I have already told you that it is essentially necessary for the good of the community that Muhammadan boys should begin their secular studies at an earlier age than they do at present.

District Boards.—The only other important matter which requires mention in connection with secondary education is the constitution of the District Boards, that have been entrusted with the entire management of Primary and Secondary education in their respective districts. It is well known that in some of the District Boards the number of Muhammadan members is zero. There is scarcely any District Board upon which Muhammadans are represented in proportion to their number. Naturally non-Musalman members do not take much interest in Muhammadan education. I am far from insinuating that they wilfully disregard Muhammadan interests. But members of a different community are not likely to comprehend properly the true interests of Musalmans and the means of furthering them. The result is that things are sometimes so managed as to prove detrimental to the interests of Musalmans. The subject is more political than educational, and I, therefore, refrain from discussing it. All that I need say further on the subject is that every effort should be made to return to the Boards a sufficient number of Muhammadans, so qualified as to be able to discharge their duties properly toward their co-religionists.

CHAPTER IX.

THE MADRASAHS.

The Madrasahs are the only institutions for the higher education of Musalmans in their classical languages. In Bengal there are four principal Madrasahs, one maintained by Government and three from the Mohsin Trust. These impart instruction in Muhammadan Law and Literature up to the high-

4

est standard prescribed by Government for such institutions. There still exist a few private Madrasahs, the relics of those noble institutions which in by-gone times were scattered throughout the length and breadth of the country. In some of these institutions Muhammadan Theology, Law and Literature are taught by eminent Maulavis, who charge no fees and devote their lives to advancing Muhammadan learning from motives of piety and religion. When Persian was the court language in India the Madrasahs were the most useful and most largely attended educational institutions in Bengal. The abolition of Persian seriously told upon their utility and popularity. With the decay of wealth and influence among the Musalmans of Bengal many of these institutions collapsed for want of funds. Some of those that still remain have a hard struggle for existence.

I have now been dealing with a subject in which I run every risk of being misunderstood. I should, therefore, premise at the outset that I am not going to denounce Madrasahs as useless institutions, which only train people who are stupid, ignorant and unprogressive. Nor am I, like some self-sufficient and opinionative people, going to laud them to the skies as the only institutions where all true knowledge has entrenched itself. Such one-sided views do not deserve much consideration. Although it is difficult to hit upon the happy mean in such a matter, yet it is very desirable to discuss the subject dispassionately with the care and calmness which its importance demands. I lay so much stress upon the subject because, to my mind, it involves matters of the most vital interests not only to Musalmans but to Islam itself. Let us calmly and conscientiously consider the following questions :—

1. Whether the Madrasahs have been beneficial to Musalmans and whether their abolition is likely to prove injurious to them and their religion ;

2. Whether the Madrasahs give the best quality of that kind of education which such institutions profess to impart ;

3. Whether the successful students of the Madrasahs find

sufficient scope for the employment of their energies and attainments ;

4. What steps, if any, should be taken with a view to increase the utility of such institutions ?

Every one who has studied the subject carefully and without prejudice, must assent to the first part of the first question. There is no doubt that the Madrasahs are doing in their way immense good to Musalmans and to Islam. Indeed they are the only Muhammadan institutions in which, in this utilitarian age, the true love of learning survives. They are untouched and unaffected by that wave of professional, technical and commercial education which has inundated not only the rest of the world but even India itself. While students in general are engrossed in thinking how they are to equip themselves with the knowledge that gives power over man and power over nature with a view to further their material interests, while all are anxious about what has been called the "bread-problem," students of the Madrasahs, true votaries of knowledge, pursue learning simply for its own sake with little prospect of worldly reward and remuneration. Are they so unintelligent, are they so foolish as not to be able to understand that the studies they pursue are not likely to help them in the race of life ? I believe they are quite conscious of the risk they run, and yet they prefer to follow a course which is likely to further their spiritual rather than their temporal interests. Under such circumstances is it possible for any educated man, whether Musalman or non-Musalman, to withhold his praise and regard from such schools and their scholars ?

I have shown while treating of the necessity of creating a vernacular literature for the Muhammadans of Bengal, what sort of Musalmans the students of our English and vernacular schools are likely to become. If the Madrasahs were to cease to exist and their students were to plunge themselves into the materialism, scepticism and godlessness which seem to be raging all around, the day will not be long in coming when Islam in India will cease to have a hold on her followers.

One day while discussing this subject with a gentleman of note, I was inclined to ridicule his opinion that if the character of the Madrasahs were to be thoroughly changed the day would soon come when there would be a dearth of qualified men to conduct even a funeral service. But after careful study I have come to the conclusion that there is some truth in this prediction. The students of our schools and colleges, with perhaps a few honourable exceptions, are so ignorant of the principles and tenets of our religion that they are not able to perform such ceremonies. Such being the state of our students in general. can any true Musalman question the utility of institutions like the Madrasahs? To sum up what I have said regarding the first question the Madrasahs, in my humble opinion, are useful institutions and their abolition would be against the true interests of Islam and its followers.

To the questions "whether the Madrasahs give the best of that education which they profess to impart and whether the successful students of the Madrasahs find adequate scope for their energies and attainments" I am afraid I shall have to answer in the negative. It seems to me that the Madrasah students are not properly qualified for any career in life. Let us see what Madrasah students do after they finish their studies. As far as I have been able to gather some of them (perhaps less than twenty per cent) are employed as teachers in Government, Mohsin and private Madrasahs, some (say five per cent) get posts as Kazis or marriage registrars, others (say other five per cent) are employed as Persian teachers in English schools, and the remaining seventy per cent are turned out into the wide world to shift for themselves as best they can. Some of them take to preaching, others to trading and some to what for want of a more appropriate term I may call begging. The Superintendents of the Madrasahs are in a better position than myself to tell you how the Maulavis employed as teachers in the Madrasahs acquit themselves. But there is no harm in giving you a little bit of my personal experience. In course of visits to some of the Madrasahs I have found that the average Maulavi (of course there are honourable exceptions) is not able to write an essay on a given subject either in correct Urdu, or in correct Persian or in correct Arabic. He teaches well books which he has studied himself but he seems to be at his wit's end when called upon to teach a book he has not read. This is perhaps due to the bad and unintelligent method of teaching already spoken of in connection with Maktabs. I should be glad to learn that I have formed an incorrect opinion. As for the Kazis, my friend, the Inspector General of Registration, will tell you how they do their work and I do not like to hazard an opinion, the accuracy of which may be questioned. As regards Persian teachers in English schools, I regret to have to say that as a class they have proved a failure. I do not mean to say that they do not know even as much Persian as is required to be taught up to the Matriculation standard. But the University now attaches very great importance to translation, and most of the marks in the second language paper are assigned to questions on translation from Persian into English and English into Persian. As our Maulavis do not know English they cannot teach translation. Moreover, many of the boys in the Mufussil schools do not properly understand explanations given in Urdu, and our Maulavis as a rule, are not able to explain in Bengali. Thus with the exception of a few who add to their knowledge of Arabic and Persian some knowledge of English and Bengali, the Maulavis prove a failure in the capacity of Persian teachers in English schools.

Are they successful as preachers of Islam? I am afraid not. To whom are they to preach Islam ? Either to their illiterate co-religionists or to non-Musalmans. In many places, especially in those where preaching is necessary, illiterate Musalmans do not understand Urdu, particularly the Persianised

Urdu of a Maulavi. So the Maulavi's preaching in Urdu is not understood by those for whom it is meant. It may not be out of place to remark here that Bengal Maulavis do not know correct Urdu. The majority cannot open their lips without breaking simple rules of Urdu grammar. If they were to betake themselves to Hindustan and preach there, they would, as a rule, prove a failure. In non-Musalman audiences the majority are Hindus, who understand Bengali. Our Maulavis do not know good Bengali, and their village dialect is not able to express their thoughts on religion. They do not know English and cannot preach to English-speaking people. An Arabic scholar of Bengal, who now holds a high post in the Education Department, was one day deploring to me his ignorance of Bengali, saying that there was a large field for proselytising effort and he could have reaped a rich harvest had he known Bengali well.

It may be asked whether the majority of our Maulavis are qualified to act as preachers. Do they know properly the life of their holy Prophet and the true history of Islam ? Are they well-grounded in Muhammadan Theology ? Have they studied Hadis and Tafsir (the science of Interpretation of the Koran and the Traditions of the Prophet) sufficiently ? I need not waste time in answering these questions as the answer is well known. In short it may be said that as preachers of Islam our Maulavis are not a success.

If one were to collect statistics of the occupations of ex-students of Madrasahs one would find that a large number of them have no employment, some have to beg and others (worse still) have recourse to very questionable means of earning their bread. It is hoped that these remarks will be received in the spirit in which they are made—a spirit of earnest regret. Let me repeat, what I have already said, that I am second to none in my regard for some of our Arabic scholars who lead religious and pious lives, and are worthy to be ideals to every true Musalman. But this is no reason why we should be blind to the faults of others. The experience of many of those who pose as champions of the Arabic scholars is confined to their own towns or to a few places outside. But I have had occasion to go to almost every leading village in East Bengal, which possesses the largest number of Arabic scholars in this province. I have had more opportunities than others to see these men in almost all the circumstances in which they are placed. I hope you will do me the justice to believe when I say that I have seen with my own eyes Maulavis shedding tears when brought face to face with starvation. Some of them are compelled to become a burden upon their community, and this may be regarded as synonymous with beggary. But beggary is certainly better than fraud. I am aware of cases in which unlawful marriages have been legalised, divorced wives have been taken back by their husbands on *Futwas* given on receipt of bribes. A new line, and a very lucrative line, has been followed by some, who have assumed the dual character of Pir and preacher. It is painful to see how some of these men wantonly play with people's faith and trifle with the Prophet's religion. Of course there are honourable exceptions. A very striking instance of fraud once came to my notice. Two Maulavis one day made their appearance at a village in an eastern district and gave out that one of them was a Hanafi and the other a Wahabi. Within a short time both of them managed to get a large number of followers. Then a meeting, very largely attended, was held to discuss and determine whose creed was true. A warm discussion ensued; one proving victorious, and the other calmly acknowledging his defeat. A large sum was given by his followers to the triumphant Maulavi, and both of them left the village. Sometime after it transpired that both the Maulavis belonged to the same sect, and that they had formed a plot to earn some money, which, of course, was equally divided between them. I would not have thus exposed the Maulavis of Bengal before gentlemen from Hindustan, had not their part of the country contributed a fair number of these Pirs and preachers. My object is not to paint these men in black colours, but simply to show to what straits they are driven and what harm they do to Islam and its followers. "Necessity" as the proverb goes "knows no law." Unable to procure a livelihood by fair means they are forced to have recourse to unfair and questionable means. Their untoward circumstances compel them to do things which they would not otherwise do. For this I would not blame these poor helpless men. They deserve pity rather than blame. It is the community that is to blame. I shall appeal to the Musalmans of Bengal, with all the emphasis at my command, to do their best to better the condition of Arabic scholars, to give them the kind of education they require—an education that will make them useful to their community and to their religion,—and to create fields for the employment of their energies and attainments. And I hope however feeble my appeal may be, it will not fail to produce the desired effect.

Let us consider the last question. "What steps, if any, should be taken with a view to increase the utility of the Madrasahs?" Some time ago when my study of the subject was not so complete as it is now, I was of opinion, that Geography, Modern History, Science and kindred subjects and the English language should be introduced into the Madrasahs, curtailing the course in Logic, Philosophy and similar subjects. It seemed to me a matter of regret that our Arabic scholars should be ignorant of such useful subjects, and that they should waste their time in learning the old exploded theories of Aristotelian Logic and Philosophy. It seemed desirable to me that in this *age of action* those metaphysical branches of philosophy which lead minds into quibbling and cavilling should be done away with and the teaching of Logic should be kept within its legitimate bounds, for, to go beyond Sharhi Tahzib and Qutbi is simply to indulge in the logical quibbles of the schoolmen. After further study and deliberation, and discussion with some of those who are in a position to express an opinion on the subject, I have had to modify my opinion to a great extent.

It does not seem possible to combine to any great extent a modern or secular education with a scholastic and more or less ecclesiastical one. Boys go to the Madrasahs to study Muhammadan Literature, Philosophy, Religion and Law and I would provide them with the highest teaching available on these subjects. It is not desirable to teach them something of everything but they should be taught everything of something. It is not advisable to overload their minds, to cram them with all the knowledge under the sun. On the contrary, it is desirable that they should be thorough masters of, and experts and specialists in, the particular subjects they choose to study. It is desirable that our Arabic scholars should be well acquainted with the different schools of Arabic Logic and Philosophy with which Arabic Literature is inseparably bound up. I do not, however, doubt the desirability of teaching modern science and Philosophy. And this raises the question whether it is not desirable to have a bifurcation of the Madrasah course of studies at some particular stage. In this connection it should be ascertained how far in the Madrasahs of Arabia, Egypt and Turkey the studies of Aristotle and Plato have been discarded and how far modern science and Philosophy have been introduced into them. Perhaps it is desirable to teach modern Science, if introduced, through the medium of Urdu. The question of suitable text-books will then arise. I doubt if these exist at present. In this connection it may not be undesirable to petition some of our native princes, say His Highness the Nizam of Hyderabad, to establish a *college for translation* similar to that which existed in the days of the Abbaside Khalifas of Baghdad, when they attempted to transplant Grecian science into their land.

The question of English, however, stands on quite a different footing. I have already shown how for want of some knowledge of English, our Arabic scholars fail as teachers and preachers of Islam, and cannot find a sufficient field for the employment of their energies and attainments. I shall

4 A

now try to show how Islam suffers on this account. Christians have gigantic missionary organisations. They spare neither money nor energy for the spread of their religion. But Islam has no organised mission of its own. Yet it has made very great progress. It presents a very favourable contrast to Christianity and other religions. One should not compare the Islam of to-day with the Christianity of the present time. Such a comparison is unfair. Islam is at the beginning of its fourteenth century whereas Christianity is at the end of its nineteenth—a difference of about six centuries. Indeed Christianity in the fourteenth century was found almost nowhere except in Europe whereas Islam, without the aid of organised missions, has spread over the wildest and most inaccessible regions in Tartary, China, Japan, Burmah, Africa and other countries. Wherever Islam and Christianity have come into collision, you know what the result has been. My object is not to disparage the religion of the Prophet of Nazareth for whom every true Musalman entertains the highest regard, but my object is simply to show what a proselytising power Islam has. If the Musalmans were to organise regular missions I verily believe that a time would soon come when Islam would find its way into all the countries of Europe and America.

According to the last census the Musalman population of India amounted to more than fifty-seven millions while the total Musalman population of the world has been roughly estimated at about two-hundred millions. As Indian Musalmans form so large a portion of the Muhammadan world would they not be justified in being the first organisers of missions to different parts of the world. The Arabic scholars would make excellent apostles if properly trained. This is not the place to discuss such a subject. I have, however, thought it proper to touch upon it in connection with our Arabic scholars, so as to attract the attention of Indian Musalmans to this important subject.

If you look from another point of view you will find how

greatly Islam is suffering for want of a knowledge of English in our Arabic scholars. Some people have taken it into their head to vilify Islam and its Prophet. Opprobrious epithets have been heaped upon the devoted head of the Prophet and deliberate lies have been fabricated with regard to his religion. I could have cited instances of a serious nature had not the procedure of this assembly forbidden such a course. When a speech is delivered or an article is written against Islam it travels with the rapidity of electricity from India to Europe and thence to America. Who is to give the lie to such assertions? Certainly none but the Musalmans. But Musalmans, who would have been by their knowledge of Islam in a position to contradict such unfounded assertions, are not even aware that such things are taking place. Those who know English and happen to read such speeches or articles are not sufficiently acquainted with the theology, traditions, and literature of their religion so as to be able to defend it. Thus what is said against Islam goes uncontradicted and is believed as gospel truth not only by the English-speaking people of the world but also by English-knowing Musalmans who are not well-grounded in the principles of their religion. I believe I have, to some extent, succeeded in proving that a knowledge of English by our Arabic scholars would do great good to Islam. If our religious books were translated into English, they would give a true idea of Islam to the English-speaking people and remove the wrong impressions which now exist. Under these circumstances I would strongly urge the introduction of English into the Madrasah curriculum.

It is also worth considering whether the standard in Arabic Literature and some other subjects should not be raised. As for Hadis and Tafsir, it is essentially necessary that these should be taught in the Madrasahs. If on the ground that these subjects are purely religious, they are not taught in the Calcutta Madrasah, which is a Government institution, there seems to be no reason why they should not be taught in Mohsin and private Madrasahs. The Dacca, the Chittagong and the Hugli Madrasahs are maintaind entirely out of the endowment made by Muhammad Mohsin, whose intention perhaps was more to give religious than secular education. With reference to this it may be considered whether in view of raising the standards in some of the existing subjects and of adding some new subjects, it is not desirable to add a fifth year class, if not a sixth year class, to the Arabic Department of the Madrasahs. My proposal is a very modest one, viz. that the course of studies prescribed for the Madrasahs be revised with a view to make such changes as may be deemed necessary. I shall not specify the line of reformation nor shall I propose what subjects and standards should be prescribed. These details may be determined by a conference of experts, and I would beg to suggest that such a conference be convened.

CHAPTER X.

HIGH ENGLISH EDUCATION.

I shall first show by statistics what progress the Musalmans have made not only in higher education but also in all kinds of education during the last decade. In 1889-90 there were in Bengal 4,33,653 Muhammadan pupils in all classes of schools known to the Department, and their percentage to the total number of pupils was about 29·0. In the year 1898-99, the last year of the decade under review, there were 4,52, 298 Muhammadan pupils, showing an increase of 18,645 pupils of this community. But the percentage of Muhammadan pupils to the total number of pupils came down to 27. Although during the intervening years there were fluctuations owing to scarcity, inundation, cyclones and other causes, over which there could be no control, there has been, on the whole, a gradual rise in the number of Muhammadan students. The fact that a rise in the total number of Musalman pupils does not produce a rise relative to the whole population shows that while Musalmans have been progressing other communities have not been standing still. The consequence is that although the Muhammadans have been making perceptible improvement, they have not been able to regain lost ground.

Much confusion arises from taking statistics of all kinds in a mass. Muhammadans form almost 33 per cent of the population of Bengal and though the total percentage of Muhammadan pupils approaches this figure, it falls off sadly in the higher branches of the educational system ; in collegiate education their backwardness is most lamentable. The question of the spread of English education among Musalmans should be extricated from this confusion. If the figures for all classes of institutions be analysed it will be seen that during the last year there were 413 Muhammadan pupils in Arts colleges, 10,728 in High English Schools, 10,569 in Middle English schools, 10,741 in Middle Vernacular schools, 41,772 in Upper Primary schools, 2,97,252 in Lower Primary schools, 82 in Professional colleges, 404 in Technical schools, 20 in Training schools, 2,938 in Madrasahs and 73,239 in Private institutions most of which are Koran schools and pure Maktabs. The percentage of Muhammadan pupils in these institutions was 3·6, 10·1, 14·09, 15·7, 18·9, 28·8, 15·3, 12·9 and 98·6 respectively. The last figure clearly shows that the private indigenous schools in Bengal are almost all Muhammadan, and the number of such Hindu institutions is next to nothing. From this it is evident that almost all the Hindu students are educated according to the recognised system of instruction whereas a large number of Muhammadan students still pursue the old method. It is, however, satisfactory to note that during the decade under review the number of Muhammadan pupils in indigenous schools has decreased by 20,819. This shows that these schools have been gradually shaking off their traditional policy and adopting the Departmental course of study, the utility of which has long been admitted but not followed on conservative grounds.

As regards the success attained by Muhammadan candidates at the different examinations, marked improvement both in quantity and quality has taken place in almost all the Departmental examinations. But the results of the University examinations are not so encouraging. In the year 1889-90, 3 Muhammadans passed the M. A. Examination, 21 passed the B. A. Examination, 57 passed the F. A. Examination, 125 passed the Entrance Examination, 418 passed the Middle Scholarship Examination, 667 passed the Upper Primary Examination, and 2,696, passed the Lower Primary Examination. During last year the number of successful Muhammadan candidates at these examinations was 2, 23, 68, 203, 728, 1,337 and 7,261 respectively. The precentage of successful Muhammadan candidates at these examinations last year was 3·1, 5·5., 6·3, 6·8, 12·9, 18·0, and 17·9 respectively. In the year 1896-97, the last year of the period for which a quinquennial report has just been published only 14 Muhammadans passed the B. L. Examination out of a total of 204, only one Muhammadan passed a medical examination out of a total of 237, and none passed any of the Engineering examinations at which 21 candidates of other religions were successful. In all the departments of learning, Arts, Law, Medicine and Engineering, the Muhammadans have fallen far short of the standard of success which they should have achieved. The higher the standard of education the more marked is the backwardness of Muhammadans. Even according to the highest rate of progress yet achieved by Muhammadans more than half a century will be required to raise the percentage of Muhammadan Graduates and Under-Graduates up to the proportion gained by Hindus relatively to population. This fact should always be borne in mind by Muhammadan educationists.

Some important steps have been taken for spread of high English education among Muhammadans These are (*a*)

Relaxation of age limit; (*b*) Establishment of Boarding-Houses; (*c*) Award of scholarships and free-studentships; (*d*) Aid from the Mohsin Fund; and (*e*) Appointment of Muhammadan officers.

Age Limit.—On my appointment as Assistant Inspector of Schools I found that the Departmental Circular in which it was laid down "that no boy who has attained the age of fourteen years should be admitted to any class of a Government High school below the fourth," debarred some Muhammadan pupils from entering high English schools. I pointed this out to the Director of Public Instruction specially drawing his attention to the fact that Muhammadan boys generally join schools later than Hindu boys, as they have to go through a course of prior religious instruction at home. The rule was accordingly relaxed in the case of Muhammadan boys.

Boarding-Houses.—One of the steps required to be taken for the proper training of Muhammadan students is the establishment of boarding-houses. The Maktabs and vernacular schools are located not only in towns but also in villages, whereas the English schools are found only at the district and sub-divisional head-quarters. When Persian was the court language most of the Government officials and members of the Bar were Musalmans and a large number of Muhammadan students used to board and lodge with them. To feed and otherwise help a *Tàlib-i-Ilm* (student) is considered a sacred duty among Muhammadans. A well-to-do Musalman considers it a social obligation to support some students. With the abolition of Persian as the Court Language the number of Muhammadan officials and lawyers fell off considerably. The students supported by them were thus put to great hardship. This is probably one of the causes that have operated to deter Muhammadans from sending their children to English schools. Even rich parents who can afford to pay for board and lodging hesitate to send their children to head-quarters stations for want of proper guardians. I made a strong representation on the subject, and the Director of

Public Instruction issued a circular in which he said, "If it is desired to build a cheap boarding-house Government may be expected to contribute towards the cost but the chief share would have to be borne by local subscribers......One of the Muhammadan teachers of the school would probably be the most suitable person to put in charge of the hostel, and he would be entitled to the ordinary capitation fee of 8 annas a head monthly." Effect is gradually being given to this circular. The Government of Sir John Woodburn, who, within his brief term of office, has given unmistakable proof of his sympathy with the Musalmans as well as with all other nationalities, has wisely decided to help only those who help themselves. It reflects very great credit upon the Musalmans of Backergunge that they have already collected a large amount for a Muhammadan boarding-house at Barisal, and His Honour the Lieutenant-Governor has kindly given a grant of Rs. 5000 for this purpose. I am, however, sorry to say that Mymensingh with a fair number of Muhammadan Zamindars, perhaps the largest in any one district of Bengal, has not yet succeeded in collecting the amount required for the purpose. It is very desirable that in this and other districts of Bengal regular efforts should he made for the establishment of Muhammadan boarding-houses.

The success of a boarding-house chiefly depends upon its proper management. An ill-managed boarding house is a hot-bed of evils. But the advantages of a properly managed institution of this kind cannot be overrated. The advantages of boarding-houses and particularly of boarding schools should be explained to the people. They do not now seem to appreciate them properly. In ancient times this was, perhaps, the prevailing system of education in this country. The Hindu Tols, the Buddhist Viharas, and the Muhammadan Khanqahs were all boarding schools. In those ancient Oriental seminaries the pupils resided with their preceptors and were not only taught free but were also fed and clothed at public expense. In those institutions undivided attention was paid to studies religious and moral lessons were inculcated, and submission and reverence were exacted in all the relations of pupils to teachers. The result of such a system of education is well known to every student of Indian history. While it was in vogue, India produced almost all the greatest and best of her sons, who have left behind them imperishable monuments in the domains of Literature, Philosophy and Mathematics. These have outlived the social ravages and political revolutions of many centuries, and are likely to last as long as the languages in which they have been written exist. The dearth of original thinkers and writers in India at the present time under the present system of education, is probably due in part to the want of boarding schools in the country. The best Arabic scholars of the time are not, perhaps, turned out by the public Madrasahs. Those who sit at the feet of reputed Arabic scholars at Lucknow, Rampur, Aligarh and Cawnpur are perhaps our best Arabic scholars. The most distinguished Sanskrit scholars, perhaps, are not trained in the Sanskrit College, but in the Tols of Nadia, where, as in days of old, pupils reside with their teachers. I had occasion to visit some of these Tols and also some of the Burmese Kyongs in the Cox's Bazar subdivision of Chittagong. The whole atmosphere of these institutions appeared to me totally different from that of our ordinary schools. Both the pupils and the teachers are cheerful, contented, happy and devoted to their respective duties. There is no demand for fine clothes, fancy shoes, or fashionable umbrellas, nor are the impudence and insolence and vicious habits and immoral and irreligious tendencies such as vitiate the character of some of our students, met with in those institutions. Boys are brought up in such boarding schools not as princes or peasants, but as human beings. Whatever their social rank and position, all of them eat the same food, wear the same kind of clothes, sleep upon the same kind of beds, sit upon the same benches and obey the same man. What peace, what contentment, what feelings of equality and amity among equals, and of obedience and

5

reverence for superiors and for authority, are thus taught and learnt! Boyhood is the time when lasting impressions are made on the mind and when children instinctively imitate those by whom they are surrounded. When boys are kept at home they generally become as their parents are. The son of a wealthy man never forgets that he is rich, that one day he is to become owner of vast possessions, and, looking down upon education as only a means of getting bread, he neglects it. The son of a poor man, on the contrary, is always conscious that he is poor, that he cannot rise to a high position in life, and thus his ambition is nipped in the bud. The sons of immoral, dishonest or disloyal men can scarcely be moral, honest or loyal. An intelligent boy is sure to catch the contagion from his surroundings. The child is the father of the man; as the boy is trained in childhood so the man conducts himself. Early impressions cannot be easily shaken off in later life. This fact perhaps accounts, to some extent, for the religious and social prejudices and political misconceptions of young Bengal. A very important factor in European education is the boarding system. To this Englishmen largely owe their manliness of character, uprightness of purpose, sense of justice and love of truth. In English schools all the faculties of a man, intellectual, moral, and physical, are properly developed whereas in Indian schools only the intellectual side of a man is cultivated.

It is very desirable that the benefits of the residential system should be properly understood in this country and the system should be widely tried. It has been tried with considerable success in the College at Aligarh. Caste may stand in the way of Hindus but in the case of Musalmans there is no such barrier. They should, therefore, feel no hesitation in trying the system.

Scholarships and Free-studentships.—The Musalmans of Bengal have lost their wealth and influence. Various causes have combined to bring about this deplorable state of things. These are too well known to need repetition. Many Musalman boys for want of means fail to prosecute their studies. In course of my tours several deserving cases have come to my notice. Only the other day while on a visit to Diamond Harbour, I met an intelligent Muhammadan boy who has passed the Lower Primary examination and is very anxious to prosecute his studies further. Although he has got a free-studentship he has not been able to begin work for want of books, which he cannot afford. I gave him the required books and he is now preparing for the Upper Primary examination. There are hundreds of such cases. Some of these boys, if properly educated, would be an acquisition to their community. The Government has already done something in this respect. On my representation Dr. Martin, the former Director of Public Instruction whose name will long be gratefully remembered by the Musalmans of Bengal for what he did in extending and encouraging Muhammadan education in this province, issued a circular announcing that eight per cent of free studentships and the same number of half-free studentships might be granted to deserving Muhammadan students in Government and aided High English schools. Some special scholarships for successful Muhammadan candidates at the University examinations were created before this and these have proved of very great assistance to Muhammadan students in Colleges. It would not be reasonable to expect more from Government in this respect. The community ought itself to move in this matter. Although the Musalmans are no longer rich there is still among them a fair number of Zamindars, traders, officers and others who, if they curtailed the amount spent on luxuries a little, could afford to give a fair amount for this purpose. Those Muhammadans who have themselves received an English education and who occupy prominent positions in Government service or at the Bar, are expected to take special interest in the education of their co-religionists. To avoid unpleasantness I shall not give details of my experience in this matter. But I shall say that I have found some of these men as apathetic in this respect as the most ignorant and illiterate peasant. Surely it is not necessary to remind these gentlemen that there lies on them a heavy obligation to help others not only as a duty to their community but as a repayment for the assistance that most of them received when they were students, from the Mohsin Fund, established by the greatest Musalman benefactor of this province. With their experience they are in a better position than others to realise the difficulties of poor students. Muhammad Mohsin naturally expected that those who benefited by his endowment, would in their turn benefit others. The assistance they received may be regarded as a debt, if not legal at least moral, which they ought to repay. If such gentlemen were to contribute a fiftieth or even a hundreth part of their income a large sum would be collected. I shall avail myself of this opportunity to appeal to these gentlemen on behalf of poor Muhammadan students, whose interests I have to look after, and I hope such an appeal will not fail to produce the desired effect.

Great discrimination will have to be exercised in the distribution of such a fund. Only poor boys who are also intelligent and well-behaved should be helped. It is more useful from a national point of view to educate clever boys than to educate dull ones. It is better to help a clever boy in the middle class rather than a stupid boy of the Entrance class.

The Mohsin Fund.—Words fail me to describe the benefits which the cause of Muhammadan education in Bengal has derived from the endowment of Muhammad Mohsin. But for his munificence many of our Maulavis would never have been what they are and few Muhammadan officers would have been where they are. I have already given you a short history of this endowment and I have shown how at first the fund was partially diverted to a purpose for which it was not intended. In 1872 the fund was set entirely free for the encouragement of Muhammadan education in Bengal. Three Madrasahs were established, Rs. 9,000 were allotted for scholarships to be tenable by Musalmans in Madrasahs or in English schools and colleges, and Rs. 18,000 went to the payment of two-thirds fees of Muhammadan pupils in Government schools and colleges, and also to the payment of Persian teachers in these schools.

On my appointment as Assistant Inspector of Muhammadan education, I pointed out the impropriety of paying the Maulavis in Government schools from the Mohsin Fund. It was represented that Muhammadan pupils in Government schools should be regarded as having a strong claim to instruction in the language which has been officially declared to be a necessary part of their education and the systematic encouragement of which has been urged in repeated orders of Government. A Maulavi should be regarded as of equal importance with a Pandit, wherever the number of Muhammadan pupils is large enough to justify the step. This would set free a considerable amount from the Mohsin Fund for the part payment of fees in English schools, for which there is a large demand and it would remove what is regarded as a grievance. The Government took this matter into very favourable consideration and ordered that the salaries of Maulavis in Government schools, which were paid from the Mohsin Fund, should be debited to Provincial revenues. But no sooner was a large amount thus set free than another difficulty arose. In consequence of the conversion of Government securities from 4 to 3½ per cent, the income of the Mohsin endowment was considerably reduced. The income of the educational branch of the endowment at that time was, if my information is correct, about Rs. 64,000. Thus the income decreased by about Rs. 8000. In order to bring the expenditure within the reduced income the Mohsin allotment for Government schools and colleges has been reduced and those Muhammadan pupils who used to pay one-third fees have now to pay half fees. So poor are some of the boys who receive aid from the Mohsin Fund that they have had to leave off their studies on account of this increase in their school-fees. Some cases of this kind were brought to my notice at Jessore.

Had the Muhammadans made a representation to Government

the matter would have been taken into consideration. It might be pointed out that if the *Putnee* system had continued and the endowed amount had not been invested in Government securities, the income most probably would have increased instead of decreasing. It might also be pointed out that if the endowment had been in the hands of other trustees than Government it would have been invested, if necessary, in better paying securities than Government Paper. As it is a charitable Fund, from which a large number of Muhammadan students, for whose welfare Government is so solicitous, derives benefit, it would naturally be expected that any such representation would receive favourable consideration. It is perhaps not yet too late to submit such a representation praying that the interest of the Mohsin Endowment be raised to 4 per cent. It is quite possible that sympathetic and kind-hearted rulers like Sir John Woodburn and Lord Curzon will take the matter into their favourable consideration.

Muhammadan Educational Officers.—The next important question to be considered in connection with the English education of Musalmans is the appointment of Muhammadan officers in the Education Department. One of the reasons which are said to deter Musalmans from sending their children to English schools is the absence of Muhammadan teachers in them. It is well-known that Musalmans desire that their children should learn the principles of their religion and usage along with their general education. They are anxious, therefore, to entrust the education of their children to Muhammadan teachers, who even without teaching religion or morality directly, may, by way of reference and illustration, instil into the minds of their pupils moral and religious principles. But illustrations cited by Hindu or Christian teachers as models of what is good and great naturally belong to Hindu or Christian history and Scriptures. This is the reason why the presence of even one Muhammadan teacher in a school gives some confidence to Musalmans.

Coldness on the part of some non-Musalman educational

officers in encouraging Muhammadans to open schools of their own or in their locality is said to be another reason for the Musalmans not availing themselves largely of the present system of education. Moreover, there are hundreds of Maktabs imparting education through the medium of Urdu and Persian, which have neither proper organisation nor systematic teaching in them. They require the guidance of inspecting officers. If they were regularly inspected and their Mianjis were repeatedly urged to add to their course of instruction useful secular subjects, many of them would have been so re-modelled as to be very useful educational institutions. As most of the present inspecting officers do not know Urdu or Persian they do not visit institutions that have not adopted the Departmental standards in the Vernacular or English. Thus for want of Muhammadan educational officers the education of Muhammadans has suffered.

I repeatedly pointed out to the Department that by degrees the appointment of a sufficient number of Muhammadan teachers and inspectors is calculated to raise the educational status of Musalmans. The Director of Public Instruction was convinced of this. Writing on the subject Dr. Martin in one of his reports observes "one of the most depressing influences which have had the effect of discouraging the advance of education among the Muhammadan community arises from the fact that so little has hitherto been done towards giving employment to Musalman gentlemen in the Department of Public Instruction." In June 1893, Dr. Martin submitted certain proposals to Government with a view to remove what he regarded as serious drawbacks to the advancement of education among the Muhammadan community in Bengal. He pointed out that in Bengal Proper and Orissa all the thirty-four Deputy Inspectors of schools were Hindus, out of 150 Sub-Inspectors of schools only 4, and of 200 school masters only 5 were Muhammadans. In Behar, however, two of the twelve Deputy Inspectors, 5 of the 40 Sub-Inspectors and 6 of the 82 school masters were Muhammadans. He recommended that "provided candidates with the necessary qualifications are obtainable, orders should be issued to the Education Department and to District and Municipal Boards to appoint only Muhammadan candidates to Sub-Inspectorships, till such time as the Muhammadan element, in the inspecting staff of each district, is represented somewhat in proportion to its Muhammadan population. The Circle Inspectors, in making appointments to Zilla schools, should also be guided by a similar principle."

The Government acquiesced in these views and desired that Muhammadans should in future be appointed to those offices to a large extent. As, however, some of the District Boards did not act according to this desire, the Government of Bengal addressed, in September 1897, a letter on the subject to the Divisional Commissioners, to the effect that "though appointments cannot be reserved absolutely for Muhammadans to the exclusion of candidates of other religious persuasions, yet His Honour thinks where qualified Muhammadans are available they should get a preference in filling up a fair proportion of these appointments up to the number in column 5 (it gives the number of Sub-Inspectorships of Schools which should be held by Muhammadans in each district according to their proportion) of the table given above even though men of equal or even higher attainments of other religious persuasions may be forthcoming and willing to take appointments ...... if there are two candidates for one appointment, each of them possessing the requisite qualifications, the Lieutenant-Governor considers that a preference should be given to the Muhammadan candidate until the number of appointments indicated in column 5 of the statement given above are held by persons of that religion." The Commissioners were requested to inform the District Boards accordingly, and to instruct the Chairmen to state in their annual reports how far effect may have been given to the wishes of Government in this respect.

I am glad that generally the District Boards, with few exceptions, are acting according to the above instructions. Some

Muhammadan Sub-Inspectors have already been appointed. As regards the appointment of Deputy-Inspectors of schools the Government has shown unexpected readiness to appoint qualified Muhammadans to these posts. During the last four years no less than ten Muhammadan Deputy Inspectors have been appointed whereas not even one such Muhammadan officer was appointed during the previous twenty-five years. The Muhammadan community of Bengal should be very thankful to Gover nment, specially to the Director of Public Instruction on whose recommendation these appointments are made, for this favour. Though up to the present Muhammadans have not been appointed school-masters to the desired extent, something is being done in this direction also.

APPENDIX A.

	1889–90. Total number of pupils.	1889–90. Number of Mdns.	1889–90. Percentage of Mdns.	1890–91. Total number of pupils.	1890–91. Number of Mdns.	1890–91. Percentage of Mdns.	1891–92. Total number of pupils.	1891–92. Number of Mdns.	1891–92. Percentage of Mdns.	1892–93. Total number of pupils.	1892–93. Number of Mdns.	1892–93. Percentage of Mdns.	1893–94. Total number of pupils.	1893–94. Number of Mdns.	1893–94. Percentage of Mdns.
Public Institutions.															
Arts Colleges	4,582	179	3.6	5,231	293	5.6	5,285	299	5.7	5,443	286	5.2	6,240	340	5.4
High English Schools	77,430	7,960	10.1	78,727	8,265	10.5	79,009	8,408	10.6	79,781	8,687	10.8	79,463	8,605	10.8
Middle " "	62,696	8,835	14.09	61,000	8,884	14.5	60,886	9,085	14.9	62,218	9,259	14.8	63,875	8,907	13.9
" Vernacular "	69,478	10,953	15.7	67,741	10,329	15.2	62,789	9,968	15.8	64,548	10,720	16.6	64,446	10,767	16.7
Upper Primary "	1,34,443	25,430	18.9	138,199	26,688	19.3	145,725	28,550	19.5	147,539	31,644	21.4	150,436	32,238	21.4
Lower " "	9,95,238	2,78,902	28.9	977,463	271,222	27.7	1,030,237	295,622	28.6	1,031,117	295,435	28.6	1,039,555	294,838	28.3
Professional Colleges	1,326	38	2.8	1,493	52	3.5	1,062	37	3.4	1,047	27	2.5	1,157	31	2.7
Technical Schools	2,660	409	15.3	2,722	417	15.3	2,864	447	15.6	3,112	507	16.2	3,652	459	12.5
Training "	1,993	259	12.9	1,983	220	11.1	1,943	194	9.9	2,382	242	10.1	2,104	169	8.
Madrasahs	2,174	2,145	98.6	2,326	2,279	97.9	2,631	2,597	98.7	2,860	2830	98.9	2,809	2,793	99.4
TOTAL ...	13,52,320	3,35,130	24.7	1,336,886	328,649	24.5	1,392,371	355,207	25.5	1,406,067	359,637	25.6	1,413,737	359,147	25.3
Private Institutions.															
Advanced	40,109	21,958	54.5	32,090	12,683	39.5	34,862	13,865	39.7	32,727	12,072	36.8	33,303	12,299	36.9
Elementary	29,615	8,752	29.5	34,027	10,678	31.3	31,571	8,331	26.3	34,324	11,084	32.2	34,230	9,441	27.5
Teaching the Koran only	66,992	66,980	99.9	62,217	62,182	99.9	70,360	70,346	99.9	63,659	63,650	99.9	64,551	64,550	100.
Other Schools not conforming to departmental standards	2,887	834	28.8	3,723	1,236	33.2	2,801	1,098	39.2	4,279	1,042	24.3	3,446	693	20.1
TOTAL ...	1,39,603	98,525	70.5	132,057	86,779	65.7	139,594	93,640	67.8	134,989	87,848	65.7	135,530	86,983	64.1
GRAND TOTAL ...	14,91,923	4,33,653	29.06	1,468,943	415,428	28.2	1,531,965	448,847	29.2	1,535,056	447,485	29.1	1,549,267	446,130	28.8

	1894–95. Total number of pupils.	1894–95. Number of Mdns.	1894–95. Percentage of Mdns.	1895–96. Total number of pupils.	1895–96. Number of Mdns.	1895–96. Percentage of Mdns.	1896–97. Total number of pupils.	1896–97. Number of Mdns.	1896–97. Percentage of Mdns.	1897–98. Total number of Mdns.	1897–98. Number of Mdns.	1897–98. Percentage of Mdns.	1898–99. Total number of pupils.	1898–99. Number of Mdns.	1898–99. Percentage of Mdns.
Public Institutions.															
Arts Colleges	6,122	362	5.9	6,193	[illegible]	6.2	6,384	361	5.6	6,440	424	6.6	7,204	413	5.7
High English Schools	80,967	9,019	11.1	81,612	[illegible]	11.5	84,882	9,497	11.2	87,603	9,591	10.9	96,970	10,728	11.06
Middle " "	68,988	9,758	14.1	68,556	[illegible]	13.8	72,425	9,908	13.7	75,104	10,409	13.8	74,928	10,569	14.1
" Vernacular "	65,087	11,366	17.4	65,977	[illegible]	17.7	66,787	11,831	17.7	66,536	12,215	18.3	61,263	10,741	17.5
Upper Primary "	159,740	35,219	22.	160,966	[illegible]	22.0	170,819	38,261	22.4	173,104	39,314	22.7	181,897	41,772	22.9
Lower " "	1,110,385	328,453	29.5	1,144,511	[illegible]	29.2	1,137,048	324,067	28.5	1,086,511	296,464	27.3	1,110,394	297,252	26.7
Professional Colleges	1,257	46	3.6	1,823	71	3.9	1,889	68	3.6	1,981	69	3.5	2,091	82	3.9
Technical Schools	3,857	454	11.5	3,607	516	14.3	3,572	477	13.3	3,374	497	14.8	7,608	404	5.3
Training "	1,670	138	8.2	1,454	87	6.	1,770	103	5.8	1,262	17	1.3	1,264	20	1.6
Madrasahs	3,086	3,064	99.3	3,111	3,090	99.3	3,017	2,981	98.8	2,954	2,935	99.4	2,624	2,613	99.5
TOTAL ...	1,501,159	397,879	26.5	1,537,810	404,652	26.3	1,548,593	397,554	25.7	1,504,892	371,940	24.7	1,546,243	374,594	24.2
Private Institutions.															
Advanced	35,066	13,567	38.7	34,692	13,323	38.4	31,641	12,191	38.5	30,539	11,651	38.2	31,772	15,934	50.1
Elementary	32,463	7,679	23.6	32,979	7,040	21.3	30,831	6,437	20.9	31,070	5,309	17.1	31,772	4,973	15.6
Teaching the Koran only	68,737	68,731	100.	68,546	68,544	100.	59,790	59,764	99.9	55,840	55,821	99.9	56,461	56,459	99.9
Other Schools not conforming to departmental standards	4,154	1,476	35.5	2,975	735	24.7	3,920	1,073	27.4	2,474	458	18.5	2,537	338	13.3
TOTAL ...	140,360	91,454	65.1	139,192	[illegible]	64.4	126,182	79,465	62.8	119,923	73,238	61.7	122,542	77,704	63.4
GRAND TOTAL ...	1,641,519	489,333	29.8	1,677,002	[illegible]	29.5	1,674,775	477,019	28.4	1,624,815	445,179	27.4	1,668,785	452,298	27.1

APPENDIX B.

Name of Examination.	1889–90. Number of successful candidates. Mdns.	Total.	Percentage of Mdns. Among successful candidates.	1890–91. Number of successful candidates. Mdns.	Total.	Percentage of Mdns. Among successful candidates.	1891–92. Number of successful candidates. Mdns.	Total.	Percentage of Mdns. Among successful candidates.	1892–93. Number of successful candidates. Mdns.	Total.	Percentage of Mdns. Among successful candidates.	1893–94. Number of successful candidates. Mdns.	Total.	Percentage of Mdns. Among successful candidates.
M. A.	3	62	4.8	2	58	3.4	2	46	4.3	2	54	3.7	...	57	...
B. A.	21	399	5.3	12	230	5.2	14	275	5.09	23	301	7.6	26	484	5.3
First Arts	57	992	5.7	16	476	3.36	47	1,035	4.5	35	830	4.2	31	826	3.7
Entrance	135	2,156	5.8	110	1,848	5.9	85	1,712	4.9	172	2,015	5.9	134	1,946	6.8
Middle English	179	1,813	9.8	225	2,043	11.01	126	1,498	8.4	198	2,015	9.8	451	3,996	11.3
„ Vernacular	239	2,079	11.5	238	2,318	10.2	161	1,782	9.03	198	2,113	9.3			
Upper Primary	667	4,682	14.2	498	4,129	12.06	407	2,491	16.3	412	2,895	14.1	776	5,309	14.6
Lower Primary	2,696	17,614	15.3	384	16,184	14.7	2,678	18,630	14.8	2,897	17,069	16.4	3,436	20,768	16.5

Name of Examination.	1894–95. Number of successful candidates. Mdns.	Total.	Percentage of Mdns. Among successful candidates.	1895–96. Number of successful candidates. Mdns.	Total.	Percentage of Mdns. Among successful candidates.	1896–97. Number of successful candidates. Mdns.	Total.	Percentage of Mdns. Among successful candidates.	1897–98. Number of successful candidates. Mdns.	Total.	Percentage of Mdns. Among successful candidates.	1898–9[illegible]. Number of successful candidates. Mdns.	Total.	Percentage of Mdns. Among successful candidates.
M. A.	5	52	7.6	4	83	4.8	1	63	1.2	1	83	1.2	2	63	3.1
B. A.	17	416	4.	18	294	6.1	14	314	3.8	22	391	5.6	23	416	5.5
First Arts	59	1,162	4.9	51	1,015	5.0	52*	1,017	5.1	66	1,281	5.1	68	1,084	6.3
Entrance	153	2,293	6.5	141	2,308	6.1	241	2,8[illegible]	8.3	178	2,721	6.5	[illegible]03	2,979	6.8
Middle English	496	4,316	11.4	472	3,931	12.0	598	4,7[illegible]8	12.6	441	3,780	11.6	728	5,63[illegible]	12.9
„ Vernacular															
Upper Primary	685	4,549	15.0	1,035	6,065	17.0	1,160	6,69[illegible]	17.3	1,132	6,972	16.2	1,337	7,437	18.
Lower Primary	5,051	26,153	19.3	5,721	31,408	18.2	7,557	38,31[illegible]	19.7*	8,738	41,941	20.8	7,261	40,579	17.9

* Exclusive of private students and teachers.